To Linda !

3 SECONDS IN BOGOTÁ

WORLD WILD TRAVEL TALES

what would you have done?

MARK PLAYNE

3 SECONDS IN BOGOTÁ

The events of

3 Seconds in Bogotá

culminated in the Colombian
capital city of Bogotá
in early June 1994.
A true story.

How long is a second?

3 SECONDS

I KNEW IT WOULD HAPPEN. Everyone had said it would. The travelling truism of the early 90s was that if you backpacked around South America for any length of time, you'd most probably return home with a story of having been robbed. The only question was, to what degree? Basic theft and a missing backpack? Mugged at gunpoint? Or caught in a bus hold-up involving trigger-happy bandits who had shot a passenger or two just to prove they were serious? It was all possible.

These stories became the currency of many a late night tale that kept us back-packers not only entertained, but served as badges of honour for those that had survived, and as maps of survival for those listening. We quickly learnt that running away, fighting – or resisting in any manner – could be a fast-track to an early grave. That attempting to outsmart thieves by not carrying cash, could in itself cause rage and provoke an attack.

Having absorbed these tales, as a precaution I carried three lots of money. The first a visible moneybag, designed to be happily surrendered at the first sign of trouble. The second batch of cash lived in a slim money belt under my belt-line. Thirdly – the real reserve with passports, traveller's cheques and cash – was hidden deep inside my trousers within a custom-made secret pocket. It would not be noticed in a normal pat-down search and could only be accessed by undoing my belt and dropping my trousers. Since I never wore underwear, I figured this acted as a built-in safety device.

Imagining the possible robberies, I rehearsed reactions.

Situation A. Someone appears in front of us waving a knife.

Plan of action. Throw them the outer money belt. Maintain eye contact. Walk backwards.

Situation B. Find myself staring down the barrel of a gun.

Plan of action. Slowly undo money-belt. Drop it to the floor. Keep hands visible and held away from pockets. Keep girlfriend behind me. Walk backwards slowly. Remember, don't turn. Don't run. Keep eye contact.

Situation C. Bus gets held up.

Plan of action. Don't speak a word. Don't make eye contact. Act like locals. Mingle and dissolve. Be invisible. Offer up second money belt before asked. Do best to keep trousers on.

I had it all worked out. I liked to be ready for the unexpected.

For the last six months, Luciana and I had travelled through Argentina, Brazil, Bolivia, Peru, Ecuador and Colombia. In terms of highway robbery, hold-ups or even good old-fashioned boring theft – nothing had happened. Zilch. Nada.

Our trip was almost over and we were due to return to Britain with nothing more than a bag of gifts and a stack of treasured memories.

We were three days away from the laughter of friends and a pint of black stout at my local pub. I visualised walking to my mother's country cottage. The dogs racing out to greet me. My mum welcoming her wayward son home with arms held out wide. The wafts of her home-baking. A pot of tea being poured. The lavender and rosemary of an English garden in the early summer bloom. Her face reacting with mock shock to the already censored highlights of our travels. The texture of the digestive biscuits, that if she wasn't looking, I might dare dip in my tea. I was almost home. I could feel it.

Yet, here I was, frozen with fear – sitting in the passenger seat of a taxi after midnight in the dark back streets of some South American city, staring at a long shiny knife blade being held to the throat of our taxi driver.

Even if something like this had been expected – even if I had absorbed the fine detail of a hundred or more stories, gleaned from the travelling grapevine – this was different to all the scenarios that had played out in my head. This situation had no label, no direct link to any memory and cause of suitable reaction. This moment in time was unique and totally unexpected.

We were in deep trouble.

Surrounded by at least eight men, who were reaching for the door handles of our taxi.

Maybe there were ten?

More were appearing from every side.

I calculated how long it would take until the car doors were open and we reached the point of no return.

Three seconds.

Then it was 'Game Over'.

If cats have nine lives, how many do humans get?

I didn't know but I decided this was the time to use one up.

Then, there it was.

'IN CASE OF EMERGENCY BREAK GLASS'.

The casing shattered.

I hit the pause button.

A twitch under my eye.

Time immediately slowed down to a snail's pace. My mind no longer had the need to race. The image of the knife in front of me lingered lazily, moving frame by frame. Relieved from the normal boundaries of time, I had what seemed like hours to shift through a lifetime of experiences, to search the memories hidden deep, for any clue that might offer a solution.

I just had to remember one thing, although time can be slowed down, it can never be stopped. I needed to keep an eye on the clock, as the blade, every now and again, would slip a frame forwards – one step closer to a very uncertain, and maybe, very short future.

A calm voice echoed within.

Right, boy. Breathe deep, relax. Listen.

Here is the plan.

Step one – In case of emergency break glass and press pause.

Yeah, I already did that... Tick! Done.

Good.

Step two – Think.

To make sense of this situation commence with the basics. Start right from the beginning and go through all the events leading to this precise moment. When is this? Who are you with? Why are you here?

Search through your memories for significant, or even vaguely similar events and work out any connections that might help save you.

Lay all your cards on the table and study them closely. Each and every happening in your life has been a tool for this moment.

Find the pattern.

Step three – Act.

Take action on what you've come to realise.

Got it?

Yes. I think so. One question.

Tell me.

Who are you?

I am you and you are me.

Huh!?

I've always been here, you're normally too busy to hear me. Consider me, as your 'in case of emergency' instruction manual.

Ask the right questions and the answers will come.

Sift through with a fine-tooth comb until the solution is found.

Or, until our time is up.

Remember, there is only one rule.

'Never give up'.

Got it?

Alright.

Good.

Right. Ready?

Yep.

2.9 seconds of real time left.

Go!

2

1994

IT WAS towards the end of May 1994. The Red Hot Chilli Pepper's recent hit 'Under the Bridge' still played hourly on radio stations.

A few weeks before, Ayrton Senna's steering had failed on the corner of the San Marino Grand Prix, causing him to plough head-on into an unprotected wall. The nation of Brazil, as well as the world of sport, were reeling in shock from their champion's death.

Affecting me more personally, Nirvana's Kurt Cobain had recently been found dead – a shotgun in his hand. He'd died on the 5th of April. With barely a couple of weeks separating our days of birth, his death hit me in a curious way. The age of twenty-seven owned a desolate feeling. An overwhelming sense that I'd completed a life cycle as if I'd been through everything already. Would the same situations simply repeat in different ways, forcing me to learn the same lessons over and over? Was life to endlessly replay the same tune? Was my destiny to marvel at life's complexities as if a song – with time, learning to pick out each instrument, melody and beat?

Was there a connection to the many rock stars who had also died at twenty-seven? Not just Cobain, but Jimi Hendrix, Janis Joplin, Brian Jones and Jim Morrison as well. Perhaps they had experienced the same sensations, of sensing nothing new on the horizon. To be clear I wasn't feeling suicidal, however, I was mourning for the loss of something that I couldn't put my finger on.

Another loop came to mind. My favourite school track event had been the 1600m, made up of four circuits of the 400m athletics track. I recalled my tactic used, where I'd initially stay back and pace myself. The first couple of laps were for warming up. Only on the third did it become time to lengthen the stride and work hard, to catch up on the heels of the leader. The sound of the bell, signalling the last circuit, was the cue to open up the legs and give it all that was possible. If life started after leaving school, I consoled myself by thinking of twenty-seven as being lap one. It was time to sit back and enjoy the ride, even if life was to become an ever-increasing spiral of repetitions.

But did the universe have a different plan?

Kurt Cobain entered the world three weeks after me. Was it to be that I'd die barely six weeks after him? Could it be my fate, to join the twenty-seven club? I succumbed to the thought for a second and came to my senses. Unable to play three chords on a guitar, I'd never released a record and couldn't even sing.

Cobain was a living legend before he died, and now dead, was an immortal legend.

He'd already done all that he came to earth to do. I'd achieved zero.

I needed a couple more laps of the track. I was still working things out.

A grown man, but full of basic confusions.

I knew everything, and yet I knew nothing.

Was I going to duck out of the race after lap one?

No way.

Besides, I'd made the promise.

Never give up.

And here I was, staring down the blade of a knife.

In the back alley of a strange city.

The short stubble on the taxi driver's cheek reminded me of a forest after a fire.

Jet black and dirty.

Veins stood out on his neck, yet they were not pulsing.

Older than me, probably late thirties.

Calm enough that I figured he'd been through this before.

His eyes resigned to his fate.

Did he even care which way this went?

Had he already achieved his life goals?

Made a number-one hit record?

Did he even have dreams?

His indifference wasn't helping me.

I needed him to want to live.

Time slipped forward one frame.

The blade tilted a fraction, making it glint.

Our lives depended on his survival instinct.

Yes, 'our lives.'

I was not alone.

LUCIANA

I MET Luciana in London's Leicester Square during the summer of 1992. I was street-selling with a box of jewellery that I opened up and balanced on the top of rubbish bins. She was a street dancer who cast spells on men, rendering them semi-senseless as she performed to the music. Half Incan Indian and half Mestizo – the name given to the lighter-skinned offspring of the Spanish settlers who'd mixed with the Ecuadorian locals – her skin was milk-chocolate and her hair long, thick and black.

She'd team up with the buskers of London. Her hips would gyrate, her short skirt losing the effect of gravity as she spun and twirled. While hypnotising the crowd with her salsa, she maintained eye contact. Like all buskers, she knew once the performance finished, people would soon melt away to avoid tipping.

Her trick was to 'bottle' – holding out a hat for donations – as she danced around the horseshoe curve of watchers. Pound coin after pound coin was popped into her hat to keep her dancing legs moving, and covered in a fine film of sweat, she'd not stop until exhausted.

Once the show ended, the money would be divided equally between her and each musician. In twenty minutes, she could rustle up more than I could bring in selling jewellery on my luckiest twelve-hour day. Although dependent on the buskers' raucous free-form music, the musicians' income rocketed when Luciana joined them and danced. Together they worked in literal harmony.

One of Leicester Square's buskers, who had a distinctive scar on each cheek, openly claimed he'd be famous one day. Even though talented, Luciana and the other buskers had gently mocked his confidence, but were now proud as Seal topped the music charts.

Once Luciana had completed a few sets, she'd flaunt past the jewellery sellers, sipping from a chilled bottle of white wine crudely disguised in a brown paper bag – a habit from her underage drinking days in the USA.

She teased for a living. She teased not only the customers who threw money at her but she also teased the buskers, jugglers and street sellers – the men who 'worked' Leicester Square. Although obviously more than a handful – I'd found myself particularly vulnerable. Friends had cautioned me, yet resistance had proven temporary and futile. In fact, the warnings only added to the attraction of this wild Latin creature. Plucking up the courage, I asked her out. On several occasions in fact. She accepted every time, and with each date stood me up, leaving me alone on a park bench holding another chilled bottle hidden in a brown paper bag. White wine which I didn't even like. I wondered if this was some kind of test.

Maybe she simply had a magic number thinking, 'If he asks me out three times, then he's worth it'? Forced to presume she needed me to ask her five times, I tried. Then six. Then seven. Perhaps something was wrong with a meeting in the park? Maybe something was not right with the cold bottle of wine? I tried upping the stakes and meeting her in a pub. Then a posh wine-bar. Only to get the same result. Slowly and reluctantly, I started to realise, I was being led on a song and dance.

As the summer wore on, Luciana vanished, apparently having gone home to Puerto Rico. Now at peace, my focus changed, and I became aware of the other beauties around me.

Leicester Square – full of the talent of the buskers, the skill of the street performers and the roguish charm of the fly-pitchers – seemed to be a magnet for the girls of Europe, sent to au pair in London. Some would buy our jewellery and instead of parting ways, would stay and help us sell. Others would help us look out for the police, who if spotted, would cause us to seemingly vanish into thin air. They called us fly-pitchers because like flies, we never rested in one place for long. Some street-sellers would hide in the back entrances of the West-End theatres. Others leant on public phones and pretended to make calls. Some of us slid our selling-boards into secret hiding places, then lit cigarettes as we dissolved into the throngs of tourists – patiently awaiting the all-clear.

Some of the girls would accompany us to our hideaway, the Imperial Pub, the fly-pitchers' zone of safety where we retreated in confidence. The landlord had forbidden the constabulary from entering his private property and many a mini-police chase ended on the pub doorstep.

The jewellery-selling riff-raff of Leicester Square made

great customers worth protecting. His only clientele who apparently drank more were the Triad gang from the neighbouring China Town. It was also here in the Imperial Pub, that we could be found, once our pockets filled with enough earnings for us to call the daily game of cat and mouse quits, park our jewellery boards in the pub's entrance, and like the other revellers of Leicester Square, enjoy the evening.

During those summer months, two lovely ladies discovered that although we were all single, things had overlapped. On this night they had me pinned to the bar – one to my left, the other to my right. However hard I tried to explain, they were not grasping my logic and lost for words, I was being out-reasoned. It was at this moment that Luciana, having returned to London, entered the bar and took in the situation. Our eyes met. A small black cloud appeared over her head. She stormed over, glared at both the girls, and yanked me away.

"He's mine," she growled.

I'd found a way to her fiery Latin heart – jealousy.

From that day on, she rarely let me out of her sight and I was forbidden from talking to non-vetted women. It was tough. The other sellers joked that I'd met my karma. Luciana had the most amazing smile and the most fearful frown. Even though I was like a wild bird with my feathers clipped – each time she laughed or danced, I was reminded that the suffering was worth it. In awe of her talent, fascinated by her culture, I'd fallen under her spell – and it soon became known that we were together. Exotic Latin Luciana became my lass.

A great friend and fellow fly-pitcher Jinxy, who had earned his nickname by his incredible luck in impossible situations, came up to me with a worried look on his face.

"You do realise. That when this new bird of yours dances. Everyone. I mean all the blokes. They can see her knickers?"

All I could do was nod and smile meekly.

And here I was, two years later.

In a notoriously dangerous city.

Late at night.

Down a deserted back street.

In the front seat of a taxi.

With Luciana in the rear.

The driver had his window wound down.

A knife being held to his throat.

We were surrounded by zombie-like men.

The butchers of Bogotá.

Coming for us.

My dream had become our nightmare.

DREAMING OF SOUTH AMERICA

SOME DREAMS ARE like magnets that pull at us with invisible forces.

We align everything so they can be fulfilled.

Y et sometimes, as quickly as we make our carefully laid plans, they fly apart, appearing seemingly unachievable.

The shapes and contours of the South American continent on maps had intrigued me since a child. As I grew older, watched films, read books and absorbed the happenings in the world, each country's name developed a character, that upon hearing conjured immediate and individual images of exotic adventures and possibilities. Unsure if the ongoing attraction as an adult was enhanced by the culture, history or the sheer wild nature of the landscape – I wondered if the truth could be as simple as the music, food and women yanking at me with an irresistible magnetism.

Even though I was now in the company of a crazy Latina, there seemed to be an equal and opposite force keeping me away from the land itself.

The logical way to approach an adventure is to calculate the budget and then commence the travels once the savings have materialised. A rationale born of a constant reliable income. However, the unreliable revenue of street selling, dictated by luck, weather and the seasons – was the polar opposite to the regularity of the nine-to-fivers whom we relied on.

Even though opposites, we were connected at the hip like two people either end of a see-saw. Our work started when their work finished. Our cash came in when their money went out. Our two different worlds connected during the lunch hours, after-work drinks or at weekends. When the nation of workers was at play enjoying a weekend or bank holiday, we'd be at our busiest.

On the hot days of the summer holidays, our income jumped, when the workers of other countries put on the hats of tourists and came to London to spend their hard-earned wages.

Once the autumn cold hit the streets and people covered up – their naked wrists and bare necks no longer calling for decoration – our sales dropped. Some street sellers weathered the winter and hibernated at home. Others flew like migratory birds to sunny climes, where the fruit born of lengthier warmer days was still ripe for the picking.

At the end of my first summer street selling, having not saved sufficient funds to travel South America, I headed to the Far East to work the streets of Hong Kong and Tokyo, with the hope of saving adequate funds to move on to Latin America.

I failed and ended up back in London for the next summer with less than I started out with before leaving. This became the pattern for two years running.

The third summer I met Luciana. Unable to even tap a tambourine to a consistent beat, I could not work with her musically, so to ensure we were able to travel together with ease, Luciana joined me selling jewellery.

After the summer of 1992 drew to a close, we flew to New York with plans to work our way to the southern hemisphere. We sold on the streets of New York's Broadway, then Miami and managed to get as far as Guatemala. With our funds running low, we decided to fly back to Hong Kong for the vast Chinese New Year celebrations. Things went well and again we set off towards Indonesia from where we planned to hop across to Mexico. As we moved south through Thailand and into Malaysia, we both suddenly came down with Dengue fever that kept us bed-bound for ten days. Severely weakened, we headed back north to Thailand's newly developing party island Koh Phangan where we could sell on the beach with ease, and rest until our strength returned. Then yet again, it was soon time to return to London for the upcoming summer.

Although a small part of Latin America was becoming a big part of my life, my dream of setting foot in South America was still proving elusive.

By the fourth year, I could not face attempting to get to South America by going the wrong way around the world again. Or getting halfway there. A new urge was also driving me – to reunite Luciana with her estranged father and brother.

She'd not seen either in the ten years since she'd left Ecuador to join her mother in Puerto Rico. So we flew on a one-way ticket to the bottom of the continent and landed in Argentina with just a thousand dollars between us. There was only one way out, and that involved travelling to the north, being closer to Europe, would mean cheaper flights. And as always, things were happening backwards. Other male travellers of my age often brought back a South American beauty to dazzle their parents. Instead, I was taking my Latin babe back to South America, to surprise one of her parents.

A thousand dollars would not last long or even buy tickets home. Inside my rucksack lurked what I'd nicknamed my 'street-seller traveller's cheques'. A full jewellery making kit and a kilo or so of solid silver rings. They just required cashing in, which is what we planned to do on the streets of Argentina. The only slight hitch to the plan was getting them into the country. We were required to either pay the one hundred per cent import duty or have the goods confiscated. Since we didn't have the finances for the duty, and our travelling funds were tied up in the silver, we didn't have much choice. And of course, losing it would have been disastrous.

A long queue of passengers, each waiting to press a big black button, awaited us. After a pause, each person would either get a green or red light. Green meant walk on ahead through, and red meant face questions and a search. The latter needed to be avoided.

A large reflective one-way viewing window sat high above the switch, behind which I presumed officials would weigh up each of us before triggering the green or red response. But why the big 'game show' like button? Was the surface sweat sensitive? Did the button act like a lie detector's sensor, that knew my state mind? Two small bottles of whisky leftover from the flight were empty in a surreptitious second. While I acted the nonchalance of deep boredom, hidden under my jacket folded over my forearm, I rubbed my fingers and thumbs until paper dry.

Some professional drug smugglers I'd stumbled across had explained to me they calmed themselves by imagining their contraband was something innocent. Following the wisdom, in my mind's eye I mutated the bag of silver rings into a bunch of bananas. No. That was stupid. Bananas grow in South America and importing food is illegal. Something bland and straightforward to imagine was needed. A bag of flour. No, silly. White powders get customs officials over excited.

Damn.

Then it was my turn. With a pounding heart, I managed a yawn and pushed the button with a super dry thumb.

The light didn't show a colour. Twice the wait of the preceding passengers. No, at least quadruple the wait.

Maybe my thumb was too dry?

My next casual yawn, that had been timed to be finished off chomping my lips as the light flashed green or red, became stuck. Half in and half out.

With eyes half closed and jaw partially open, stuck awaiting the light, the yawn was caught in no-man's-land.

I attempted to swallow. No good.

Then tried to cough it up.

The yawn was firmly stuck awaiting the signal.

The light blinked.

Green.

Rocking my sore jaw side to side, I ambled towards the red channel. An irritated customs officer shooed me away, pointing at the green exit. At least I'd done that bit well.

The baggage claim loomed closer. Half a dozen guards stood arms crossed, staring at anything that moved – and all that didn't. Had the silver been spotted on the airline's baggage X-ray? Were they waiting to see who picked the goods up before they made their move?

I was separated from Luciana.

My bag arrived on the carousel and I lumbered it onto my trolley as if barely bothered. The guards seemed distracted by a group of girls in early summer short skirts. The exit-doors teased from ten metres away. Was this the chance? Stifling another fake yawn, I took the first steps forward.

"*Señor.*"

The call coincided with the precise movement of my first leg. Pretending not to hear, I swung my second leg forwards, the exit now barely a few metres ahead of me. I just needed to keep moving. The voice called out again, this time twice as loud.

"*Señor!*"

Knowing turning to the call implied guilt, I played the dumb gringo and kept going.

A hand grabbed my shoulder, stopping me dead on my tracks.

The guard glared at me.

"*Señor!* Your baggage! Passport please."

The consequences of his words caused the memory of the smells of Hong Kong's streets to hit the back of my throat. Flashing neon lights filled my vision. The humid, steamy alleyways where we hid from the Hong Kong police clouded my spirit. Could I ever escape that place? The bags contained all that we owned. If confiscated, we'd have to start from financial zero again. I would be back to making earrings by twisting animal shapes out of wire. I'd been deported in a similar situation before. Incredibly, from Europe's Canaries Islands. The Official had claimed that as I'd arrived with no funds, I could not stay. My big bag of jewellery to make and sell didn't persuade him. Even a brand new credit card with two grand on it was not enough. He wanted to see cash. I suspected the real reason for the deportation, was my longish hair and the two gorgeous Italian girls with me – pure resentment. All three of us were put on the return flight to London. When back in Leicester Square the next evening, friends asked, 'Where were you last night?' When I replied 'Gran Canaria', no one believed the truth.

The Argentine guard snatched my passport from my hand and checked it against the labels on my bag.

"*Si Señor.*" He grinned, displaying a full set of ridiculously white teeth.

"Your bags."

I returned his grin, baring him my teeth. This man had no reason to be jealous, he couldn't see Luciana. Why does this have to happen to me? Why can't I set foot in South America? I should be eating Argentinian steaks and drinking red wine, not yet again back in the Far East slurping from bowls of noodles. My mind was buzzing, already anticipating the white noise of a thousand air-conditioners. Units that protruded from the windows of HK's high-rise tower blocks, stacked against each other like sardines. The cacophony produced from one of the highest density populations on earth. By flying direct to South Argentina, I thought I'd outmanoeuvred my luck. And now my luck was outmanoeuvring me.

The guard stopped smiling and repeated his words, talking slowly as if I was an imbecile.

"*Si Señor*. Your bags."

He pointed towards the exit.

"You go now."

I wasn't going to ask any questions and turned obediently and pushed the trolley towards freedom. Had I misunderstood? Then I heard him again.

"*Señor!*"

I turned.

The guard was beaming at me.

"*Bienvenido a Argentina!*"

The man with the never-ending thankless job of ensuring passengers left with only their correct luggage, was warmly welcoming me to his country.

I bowed my head to him in appreciation before shuffling through the doors into the airport's arrival lounge – dazed, slightly drunk and deliriously happy.

I'd made it.

Luciana had already found our friends. She grabbed me from behind and shouted.

"Boo!"

I jumped out of my skin.

They all seemed to find it very funny.

I didn't care. I was finally in South America. It was early December. The Argentine summer season was about to start. We had little money, but with half a bag of solid silver goodies, some of them set with gems – all we needed to do was sell them. Although I felt lucky, I was clueless to how lucky I was soon to be.

* * *

Not only had a few kilos of silver rings weighed down my bag. A complete jewellery making kit including a set of pliers, mini blow torch, soldering flux, several coils of silver wire, a full-sized hammer and topped off by the craziest thing I've ever carried – a large block of stainless steel – all added to the weight. Although a dead weight, it was invaluable as a base to beat the silver flat on, without marking the precious metals.

Buried deep in my backpack, was the most indispensable travelling accessory of all – my Swiss army pocket-knife. As a boy, upon joining the boy scouts, my father had bought me one with my name engraved on it. Then progressing from making bows and arrows to needing the tools for basic camping, I'd upgraded to a trusted larger lock blade version that could cut through a loaf of bread in a single go. The saw had melted its way through countless obstacles, the bottle opener had cracked beers from France to Australia and the corkscrew had uncorked more wine bottles than was possible to remember.

My rucksack held a few other treasured possessions that helped convert random pensions and hotels into a home away from home. A miniature pocket-sized atlas. A full collection of CDs with a player, alongside a camera, pocket computer and a prized miniature short wave radio.

When we set up a base for more than a few days, I'd rig up an extended aerial by stretching some jewellery-making wire along the gutters outside our room. Hunting for the elusive BBC's World Service, I'd often find the faint crackling signals from as far away as Africa. The legendary voice introducing the news as 'This is London', was a home comfort second only to a mug of tea, and a pint of beer. Once the BBC's World Service had enabled me to receive news ahead of the local media. It was mind-bending to think about how the information had travelled. The story left Argentina, hit the news desk in London, had been chosen for a news bulletin that was then relayed to radio stations in Africa, that was picked up via an improvised aerial in a small town in Argentina – barely half an hour from the actual location of the news. The world-service had enabled me to be the first in the area to say. "Never guess what? A massive bush fire up the road has set a petrol station ablaze. An inferno."

With something for every situation, I had little room left for clothes. On the other hand, Luciana only carried a coveted Game Boy, on which she played 'The Brick Game' incessantly to numb long journeys. Filled to the top, the rest of her bag was makeup and clothes.

* * *

The 'art of doing things backwards' struck again. Within a few months of working the streets of Argentina and Brazil, we'd saved enough for both of us to travel around the continent. The finances that had failed to materialise in the previous three years had magically appeared as if was meant to be. It seemed that letting go of the idea that substantial savings were needed to visit, had enabled the magnets to be aligned correctly. South America herself, had given us the money to travel her freely and buy our plane tickets home.

So, having worked and saved in the wealthier economies of Argentina and Brazil, we now set off to travel and spend through the poorer countries of Bolivia, Peru and Ecuador. Our plan was, once at the top of the continent, we'd fly back to England from Colombia. To arrive back in time for Britain's best-kept secret. Hidden deep in England's west country, for the week of mid-summer solstice, some of the most prominent groups of the time were booked to play in a field. This year, the stages were to be graced by Van Morrison, Radiohead and the Beastie Boys as well as some unknown bands like Pulp and Oasis. Although desperate not to leave this land of my dreams, the legendary Glastonbury music festival was not going to postpone her dates just for us. With stock required to sell, we divided our days between sightseeing and hunting for handi-crafts. Some of the jewellery would be bought ready-made, but the real fun originated in designing and ordering custom items meaning we had unique goods.

Like all back-packers, to find our way around we took our basic information from paper maps and heavy well-thumbed guide books. The king being the *Lonely Planet* guide known on the circuit as 'The Bible'. Most importantly of all, we relied on the word-of-mouth recommendations and warnings from our fellow travellers. Following these suggestions, we hopped from town to ancient ruin to handicraft village, weaving our way north.

Travelling by bus, we swung around the bends of roads perched high on the passes of the Andes mountain range, catching glimpses of the gorges and valleys hundreds of metres below. These hairpin bends were often marked with little wooden crosses. Reminders of who had taken the corner too wide to be seen alive again. We'd grade the danger by the number of memorials, referring to them as fives or eights – and wince if they hit double digits.

We wrote letters back home with rough travel plans, giving approximate dates when we might pass through certain cities. Without fixed addresses, the international poste-restante system enabled us to receive letters that the post offices would hold for us. On reaching these places, we'd eagerly queue at post offices to see if anyone had posted news from home. If lucky, we'd sit in cafés studying the handwriting and sense, even if just momentarily, familiar fragrances from the paper and ink that had been in the hands of a loved one. The mail would usually be an 'airmail-letter', a flimsy blue piece of paper that folded in three and stuck to itself, and cost an affordable set price to send. Real envelopes that might contain photographs, were the genuine treasure sent with the risk that travel plans might change, cities never be visited, and the letters never found. As a precaution when writing to friends also on the road, I'd often copy a letter three times and post it to three different cities – meaning I had three chances that it would reach the eyes of the intended.

And now, six months had passed since we'd landed in Buenos Aires on our one-way tickets.

The last town we'd passed through in Ecuador was a small Andean mountain town called Cotacachi. The air hung heavy with the musty smell of leather, the town's speciality craft. The market stalls that filled the central streets were draped with everything that could be imagined from jackets, bags and belts to wallets and key-rings. All handmade in natural tan leather, with some embroidered in bright primary colours. The Andean market women stood behind their displays each with matching long straight jet-black hair, parted in the centre into pigtails. With broad smiles under rosy cheeks, they willed us to buy.

Three days from home, I'd managed to organise all my last-minute gift-buying on one stall. A wallet for my brother, a pencil case for my kid-brother, a handbag for my sister and for my mother a uniquely designed hold-all with a zip spiralling around its girth, meaning it could be shrunk or expanded.

Luciana, however, wasn't going to let the stallholder get away with the price that I was happily about to pay.

"*Una yapa por favour?*" she grinned knowingly.

A '*yapa*' is the term for a discount, whereby instead of asking to pay less, a little extra gift was asked for in addition. A bit like a baker's dozen when thirteen are given, not twelve. A smile spread across the stallholder's face, signalling I was purchasing enough to deserve my 'yapa'. From the back of her stall, she threw me a penknife holder designed to be attached to a belt. It fitted perfectly. My ever-faithful Swiss army tool kit now owned a new home on my belt. I hoped it matched my broad leather brim hat.

Luciana grinned at me. "You look like that Indiana Jones."

Unsure if she was mocking or flattering me, I frowned.

"Or Crocodile Dundee?" she added.

Holding up a hand to cast a shadow on the ground like a sundial, I squinted at the sun and with my best Aussie accent, muttered, "Must be twenty past ten."

Both of them looked at me blankly.

I quietly packed the rest of the gifts using the gift-bag for my mother and shuffled off to see if I could find any more last-minute goodies to take home.

I now had three bags to carry, but we were nearly at the end of our cross-continental adventure. One more long bus journey over the border into Colombia, followed by an internal flight, a two-night stay in Bogotá and we would fly home.

Our bags not only contained our clothes. They held our irreplaceable travel photographs and their film negatives as well as letters, gifts and mementoes. They held the jewellery making tools and the silver that we made and sold. They also bore the stock that we'd commissioned and planned to sell. Our rucksacks were more than heavy in weight, they represented our livelihood and our future plans.

Yet, right now this baggage and the stuff they had been filled with, seemed the most irrelevant bunch of disposable rubbish in the whole wide world.

Yes, I'd fought to get these bags into South America.

But I could not have been happier to leave without them.

Our lives were handcuffed to our bags.

These people were now chained to our bags.

Our fates intertwined and inseparable.

Locked in a grim dance.

I'd planned carefully to avoid this.

I wished I could lift my arms high.

"Guys, you can have everything!"

Then walk backwards.

Luciana shielded behind me.

I was prepared for that.

I wasn't ready for this.

No-one could be ready for 'this'.
'This' was not meant to happen.
We were going to be killed.
For what?
A pair of rich-country passports?
Our rucksacks?
The clothes that we were wearing?
They didn't know about the silver.
Or about the money I had hidden on me.
But of course, they'd be finding it.
A little bonus.
Once we'd stopped struggling and become silent.
A glint as the knife blade moved.
2.8 seconds of real-time left.
Big... deep... breath.

5

THE FINE ART OF BAD SPANISH

IF GETTING to South America had taken blind determination and perseverance, the other essential part of my dream, learning the lingo, had been as easy as teaching a cow to dance the tango. The only difference being that cows don't give a damn about dancing, whereas I was keen to speak Spanish. Even if just a few words. So as not to come across as a typical lazy Brit, happy to have the world speaking his language. Which of course I was.

The primary two things we imagine we need in a foreign language, is the ability to swear and tell a joke. We think swearing makes us look streetwise. Jokes convey understanding, especially for the English, as they are how we speak the truth, confront the un-confrontable, and cope with the un-copable.

I soon learnt that '*Hijo de puta*', meaning 'son-of-a-bitch', could be used for anything and everything. Brilliant for when things went wrong, or when things went right. Superb to describe unlikable people and if the tone was slightly changed, to describe likeable people. If I stubbed a toe or burnt the cooking, it made the perfect exclamation. When confounded by something I didn't understand, the phrase combined with a little shake of the head made a convincing catch-all reply.

These three words, alongside a few variations, enabled me to swagger around with a certain level of street eloquence, but I needed more. I wanted to know how to ask for the things – like coffee, food and beer.

The previous year when selling our handicrafts in Germany we'd found ourselves amongst many South American artisans, who had also travelled to the German city streets to earn the strong Deutsche Mark. This provided me with a chance to get an ear for Spanish, while also learning a few words in German.

As that summer wore to a close, we flew to New York and sold on the streets of Broadway before driving south and discovering the promenade of Miami Beach. Hurricane Andrew had recently ripped through Southern Florida and left many seafront shops derelict. This gave us plenty of pavement space to set up our stall in front of the boarded-up windows. Although we owned no licence, Luciana with her American passport had the right to work, so she manned our little shop. I stayed indoors at our run-down art deco motel room and entertained myself by conjuring up new jewellery designs, while watching back-to-back American TV.

Miami Beach, the heart of a vibrant gay community, attracted police of that persuasion, who asked for transfers to this small, yet special part of Florida, where being true to yourself was considered natural. In this little corner of decadent bohemia we felt right at home.

To meet demands, I developed a line in erotica jewellery. There had been a fashion of little silver figures whose arms and legs were pinched to make them grip the outer ear, giving the impression of a miniature man climbing the ear. These 'little men' ear cuffs were a must-have from '90 to '92, then out of fashion by '93, and now a small bag of unsold left-overs needed a purpose. For the erotica rings, I wound a thick sprung coil out of a heavy solid silver wire to fit a finger or thumb. I soldered two of the figures to separate parts of the coil, in such a way that if the ring was squeezed, the men would appear to writhe against each other. Everyone from the café-waiters to the police snapped them up. Orders were placed with personalised variations to the style, materials and poses, and I couldn't make them fast enough.

After receiving a couple of requests for versions made in gold, I cycled on my single gear, twenty-dollar, 'probably stolen' beach bike over the bay, and into downtown Miami. In a backstreet, I stumbled across my first real Cuban café festooned in bright hand-painted signs naming various snacks and my favourite drink – a milk coffee, or café-con leche. This was my chance to try my first words of Spanish in a real situation. Stepping inside, I entered a few square metres of Cuba. Two burly looking cooks, sleeves rolled up to their elbows revealing heavily tattooed forearms, returned my broad smile with deep frowns. The waitress, elbows propped on the counter, face cupped in her hands, waited calmly for my order. They had no idea that this gringo was about to blow them away by speaking their mother tongue.

Giving a nod of recognition to the macho cooks, I offered

the waitress my friendliest smile and let the words roll off my tongue. *"Ein café con leche, bitte."*

The confusion on her face matched the disappointment in my heart. Just five words and I'd spoken three of them in Spanish, and two in German.

Languages were never my thing.

The following year we arrived in Argentina. Since few people spoke English, it was time to put my head down and learn Spanish 'I'm-back-at-school' style. A matching dictionary and teach-yourself Spanish book were soon my new prized possessions. Their slim red and orange covers represented my dreams of future eloquence. Ramming a book into each rear pocket of my jeans, they went everywhere with me – the covers soon becoming worn and battered.

I'd read somewhere that knowing one hundred words of a language meant you had the basics covered. Five hundred words made up the foundation and two thousand words earned the speaker the badge of being considered fluent.

I set my target at five hundred words. To get a head-start on this mammoth task, I trawled through the dictionary looking for words I already understood and ticked each one.

Si – yes – Tick

Non – no – Tick

Que – what – Tick

Por favour – Please – Tick

Gracias – Thank you – Tick

Señor – Mr – Tick

Señora – Mrs – Tick
Gringo – Foreigner – Tick
Vino – Wine – Tick
Color – Colour – Tick

I'd barely started, and there were ten words towards the goal.

Fantastico – Fantastic – Tick
Problema – Problem – Tick
Intelligente – Intelligent – Tick
Estupido – Stupid – Tick!

I hit some word combinations.

Café-con-leche – Coffee with milk
Chilli-con-carne – Chili with meat

Tick! – Tick! – Tick!

Soon, there were more than a hundred words marked in my dictionary as 'known'.

Then, like a coalminer finding a seam of gold, I discovered words that were the same in Spanish as English. Latin-based words that leapt off the page and were totally tickable.

Words ending in 'al' like *individual, hospital, accidental, decimal, universal* or *paranormal*.

Words ending in 'able' – *adorable, comparable, favourable, irritable, variable, biodegradable* and *inevitable*.

This was a treasure trove.

Then another batch of words, that at first glance appeared Spanish, threw off their disguises.

Words that ended in 'cion' instead of 'tion' – *determinación, dirección, devastación* and *invitación*.

Within an hour I had my five hundred words. All I needed

to do was mimic the Latin Spanish accent, and the job was done.

Learn Spanish – Tick!

But of course, I had a genuinely fluent partner who wasn't going to let her man get away with a lousy gringo accent on some Latin-based words. Due to meet her father and brother in five months, her 'European import' was expected to understand more than a few basic pleasantries.

With the diligent patience of a born teacher, Luciana began with the basic verbs.

'*Quiero, quieres, quiere,*' which is 'I want, you want, he wants'.

Pretty important stuff especially as 'I want you', or '*Te queiro,*' is how the Spanish speakers say 'I love you'.

I learnt how to ask for a tea. '*Quiero un té*'.

Remembering the small backstreet café with big macho cooks, I made a mental note to never confuse the two sentences.

* * *

Working hard, Luciana made the perfect Spanish teacher until one day after a squabble, I made a simple school-boy error. On overhearing her version of the story, instead of keeping my newfound ability to grasp the gist of a conversation secret, I jumped in and blurted out my denials, "I didn't say that. What I said was..."

I won the battle, but had blown my cover and hence the war. The next time I slid my Spanish book towards her asking for a lesson, she snapped it shut and slid it back.

"You know too much Spanish already."

A while or so later I dared to ask her how to say 'me'.

"*Me*" she replied, pronouncing it as 'Meh'.

I asked how to say 'give'.

"*Dame,*" she smiled.

Splicing the two words together now meant requesting something was easy. *Dame-me un cafe con leche, por favor* meaning give me a milk coffee please. I was getting the hang of this Spanish thing.

Many weeks later, a friend on passing me the pepper as I'd just requested, frowned. "Why did you say 'give me-me the pepper?"

I looked at him blankly.

He explained, "You always do it. You only need to say 'me' once?"

"What?"

Horrified, I confronted Luciana.

"You've heard me, for over three months, saying, 'give me-me,' every time I've asked for something?"

Barely hiding her delight, she said, "People understood you fine."

I glared at her in disbelief

She smiled. "Anyway, I didn't want you to stop saying it. I thought it sounded kinda cute. And it proves you're English."

Double whammy.

I'd confidently been getting this simple two-word phrase wrong from Buenos Aires to Cordoba, and back again. At least I'd only ever said *'Ein café con leche bitte'* once.

Unknown to me, a triple whammy was soon upon me.

One night in a small packed bar, a good friend Rafa was

mid-story with everyone listening intently when he paused and leant towards me with his arm outstretched. He came closer and closer until his face hovered just inches from mine. Without so much as batting an eyelid, he asked me. "*Dame un beso?*"

Beso meant 'a kiss'. I knew that word. It was one of the first I'd learnt. He'd asked me for a kiss. His girlfriend was sat next to Luciana. Totally confounded, and in shock, I decided to buy time and repeated his words. "*Dame – un – beso?*"

The bar erupted. Rafa motioned to something behind me. Only able to see a neat shelf of empty glasses, I was bewildered.

Once able to get his words out, Rafa explained. "I said, '*Dame un vaso*' not '*Dame un beso*.'"

He used the back of his hand to wipe tears from his eyes. "*Dame un vaso*, means pass me a glass."

That night I learnt, and have never forgotten since, that a 'V' and a 'B' in Spanish, are pronounced the almost identically.

This small bar we'd been in, was in a quaint town called Mina-Clavero set just west of the Sierras de Córdoba mountain range. A small river ran through the town whose mix of mini-canyons and sandy beaches attracted sun-seeking tourists, earning the inland town the nick-name of 'The western coast of Argentina'. Here we worked on the local artisan market for the month of January under the height of the southern hemisphere's mid-summer sun. This market became the perfect breeding ground to get a grip on the language. The customers only had a few questions and I'd hear them over and over.

How much is it? Is it real silver? Did you make it? Will you give a discount?

I soon memorised the answers. The only trouble was that due to the variety of accents, I rarely understood which question was which so would listen to the tone, watch the body language – and take a guess. If the customer received the wrong answer, they'd happily repeat the question a further two times. I'd only lose a sale on the third error as they shrugged and walked away. I'd stumbled on incentivised learning.

A pattern was also emerging. If I got the right answer, they would progress to the second question which, on having heard my accent, would nearly always be, "Where are you from?"

"*Soy Inglés,*" I'd reply, I'm English.

Due to the recent Falklands War between our respective countries, the next question was nearly always about our leader at the time, "Do you like Margaret Thatcher?"

With the non-stop incentivised repetition, I had a series of answers ready to roll off the tip of my tongue when a new customer arrived on the stall.

"Yes. It's real. Okay, a small discount. I'm English. No, I don't like her."

* * *

Rafa, just five years older, was a mix of friend and older brother, who had the patience to explain things, while also watching my back. He had sublet a restaurant perched on the rocks above the river. We spent most evenings there with him swapping stories on the outdoor terrace which had stunning views over the town's bridge and beaches. The company was delightful, the wine superb and the steaks typically huge. In Europe if we ordered a steak, chips and salad, we'd expect a plate half filled by chips, a large green salad and a small steak. Here in Argentina the standard was a steak that covered the majority of the plate, encircled by about five or six chips, a lettuce leaf and a slice of tomato.

From Rafa's terrace, we could see a mess of red bricks and the vague outline of foundations on the other side of the river. I was curious and asked Rafa what had happened

Nine weeks earlier they had experienced heavy rains. It had been a long hot run up to the summer and the earth had been baked hard and was unable to absorb any water. All the rainwater ran off from the mountains funnelled into Mina's river. The river had swelled to the point that a beach-side restaurant had been swept away. We were now looking at the foundations, all that was left. A couple of hundred metres downstream the sides of the river rose to become sheer almost canyon-like. A bridge had spanned these waters. The walls of the restaurant, having been washed away in their entirety, wedged themselves against the bridge, creating a dam. The waters unable to escape then rose so fast many people in Mina Clavero became trapped in their houses. We'd rented a room up the hill away from the river. The sixty-year-old owners of this house recounted the horror story of how they'd become trapped in their ground floor living room. The water gushed in so fast they could not leave against the pressure. They had to swim to stay afloat. The waters rose to six inches from the ceiling, then scarcely a minute or two from drowning in their own front living room, the waters receded even faster than they had risen. The owners had shown us the high tide mark on their interior walls. The extent of the flash flood was hard to believe, yet the mark was clearly visible. Not only that, the neighbours all had similar stories, each proud to show us the high water point on their property, as if showing us gave the event credibility in their own astonished minds. Our first-floor flat roof veranda was the roof of their living room. When I sat there making jewellery, it had been surreal to imagine it had briefly been an island.

The waters receded so fast when the accidental dam had collapsed under the weight of the water it had been holding back. The deluge released left no trace of a small hamlet downstream. Nine people and their houses vanished without a trace.

Once Rafa had closed up, we'd stay for late drinks before heading out to a club. One night, around the middle of January, just as the restaurant was being closed, it started to rain. It quickly developed into the kind of rain that drenched a person to the skin in seconds. Yelling as we ran for cover, I held open the door to the kitchen and ushered everyone into the dry – shouting 'Rapeeedo'. I touched Rafa's back as he passed me who recoiled in a violent gesture of frustration. Having never seen him angry, I was taken aback. The level of the river was rising fast. Within a few minutes, the water covered the beaches, quickly rising to meet and then swamp the main lower road bridge. The river thundered into it, kicking up and over angrily at the impedance. A curved torrent of water was soon the only clue left to the presence of the bridge. The waters kept rising, venturing up the rocks towards the restaurant. Racing to get everything off the floor, we placed the soft furnishings on the tables and electric kitchen items on high shelves. Within fifteen minutes, the water was ankle deep in the restaurant. Three minutes later it was knee deep. Only too aware of the risk, Rafa called for us to abandon ship and leave the restaurant for higher ground. Luciana and I stood at the water's edge on the steep road that led back up to our pension. The river pulsed rising in surges, causing us to walk backwards to the sound of women crying with fear as their determined men returned to rescue possessions from their houses. We watched one man run back to his car. As he opened the doors the water touched his tyres. By the time he had the engine started, the water was halfway up his wheels. He reversed out but the waters were now entering the car; to gasps he swung the car back deeper into the flood, so he was pointing up the hill. His wife was hysterical. He kept the engine roaring so the pressure of escaping exhaust fumes stopped water entering the engine system and then accelerated to reach the higher ground, to the cheers of the bystanders. His wife's screams didn't cease, as she now berated him without mercy.

After making sure Luciana was home and dry, I went back out and spent the rest of the night on a surviving footbridge. High above the floods I watched in awe as the brown waters surged, leaping over submerged obstacles. The incessant power of these waters had me totally mesmerised. That night the flood rose a quarter of the way towards our pension, before quietly shrinking back.

By daylight we ventured back to the river to find her again tame, snaking her way under the bridge, past beaches, now without a grain of sand.

In silence, we picked through muddy slime in Rafa's restaurant to see what could be salvaged. Eventually with a big sigh, Rafa straightened his back and threw his car keys to one of the waiters.

"We need some music. Get some CDs from my car."

Rafa met my eyes, only too aware of what had happened last night between us. We eyed each other, waiting for the other to speak.

He spoke first. "Why do all you English say *Rapeeeedo*?"

Baffled, I shrugged.

Rafa seemed in pain. "It's *Rapido*," he said, pronouncing the word as we say it in English, adding an 'o'.

Raising my shoulders just slightly, I replied.

"I think I got it from a cartoon we watched as kids. *Speedy Gonzales*?"

I'm not sure which one of us looked more bewildered.

How could a mispronunciation from a children's animation get someone so angry?

Another waiter lifted his head from mopping the sludge.

"Go on, Rafa. Tell him. He doesn't understand."

Rafa sat back onto a clean table.

"In 1982 anyone in their later teens whose identity card number ended with an even number stayed home. Anyone with an odd number was conscripted, unless their parents had the money to bribe the military. They'd get a day or two of training. Get given a gun and sent to fight your British paratroopers."

Rafa paused long enough for us to absorb his words.

"Our professional soldiers stayed at home."

We could almost hear the mud cracking as it dried.

Filling his chest with air, Rafa continued. "And I was eighteen. My ID card ended in an odd number. And my parents couldn't afford the bribe."

He shifted his weight on the table, swung his feet and stared at them as if he'd only just become aware that he'd been standing in two inches of mud.

"Anyway. I was one of the lucky ones. I ended up a prisoner of war."

He turned his eyes back to me.

"Your soldiers were nice to us. Considering."

Rafa straightened his posture.

"But when they marched us in a line. When we walked by them. They used the butts of their rifles to hit our backs. And they kept shouting '*Rapeeeedo! Rapeeeedo!*'"

He spat the words out as if he'd accidentally swallowed some river mud.

I watched my new best friend rock slightly on the table. I tried to get my head around how someone from my country had been paid to try to kill him. And he'd been forced into carrying a gun to kill my countrymen.

Rafa was one of the kindest and funniest people I'd ever met. When we'd arrived in the town on our last dollars, he'd refused to let us pay for food. Now we had money he refused to let us pay as we were now friends. It became a game to buy him drinks in return. Rafa was a big softie, not a killer. No words could express my disorientation.

Worse, I remembered how close I'd been to becoming one of the Brit Boys sent to the Falklands. Twelve years earlier I'd been following the war between Britain and Argentina as if a sports event. As a young teen, I was being educated in an all-boys grammar school priming us for the jobs in law, medicine, banking or the military. For careers advice in 1980 we plugged our details, passions and favourite subjects into an early computer that apparently, alongside our academic progress, could calculate our ideal destiny. It spat out results on holed paper that a specially trained careers adviser deciphered against a chart.

The basics of how I wished to lead my life included the outdoors, foreign travel and adventure. For a job, I'd wanted to be a vet, or a doctor.

The computer whirred away and out popped its conclusion, suggesting two jobs for me. Tank commander or male military nurse. My friends laughed as I tossed a coin to help me choose.

"Heads to blow them up. Tails to put them back together again."

The newspaper on our kitchen table had been my stepfather's *Daily Mail*, a tabloid with Britain's highest readership. This source of information cornered my view of the world and as designed, gave me tunnel-vision. Aged just fifteen, I was cutting the newspaper's headlines to stick in a scrapbook, fascinated by the lengthy articles on weapon systems. I cheered on our paratroopers at Goose Green and to my utter shame thought the sinking of the *General Belgrano* troop ship illegally outside the war zone was justifiable and all part of war. The ship had been full of conscripts.

Although we had been told the Falklands War was a territorial dispute, as I grew up and read more widely, the truth soon become apparent. The leaders of both Argentina and Britain had been very unpopular in their own countries. No prime minister in Britain had been less popular than Thatcher since the Second World War. That is until she sent her 'Task Force' to the South Atlantic to confront the 'Argies'. Within days the British people were successfully distracted from the economic woes and focussed on the new external enemy. Thatcher's ratings rocketed. Argentina's leader Galtieri enjoyed the same effect for the same reason. The war was just a publicity exercise for both of them to massage their home popularity ratings.

The British media's rabble-rousing caused queues of young men to form at recruitment offices nationwide to sign up and join the fight. Frustrated that I was too young to join them, my mother tried to calm me saying she knew lovely Argentinians. Her words washed over me. I'd consumed every word printed in the tabloid *Daily Mail* and absorbed the TV news back to back. This was a good war. My mother was mistaken. The 'Argies' needed a good kick up the backside.

The military seemed a sensible careers option, besides they even paid for university fees. I joined test flights and entered the selection process to become a helicopter pilot which seemed a more clever option than being in a tank. Helicopters were more nimble and could blow up tanks. Then at an army recruiting centre's open day, I saw the infantry proudly displaying their new shoulder missiles designed to blow helicopters clean out of the sky.

Kids learn quickly and within two years my life was changing direction rapidly. Each breath outside the education system and each word independent of the media, were reshaping my understanding. The final piece of the jigsaw was put in place when I purchased a special train ticket, called an

InterRail Pass, that bought a month's worth of free train travel in Europe. At a youthful seventeen, I'd headed out alone to explore the continent. While traversing France, I shared a compartment with a group of soldiers. When I voiced my ambitions to join them, their response surprised me.

"Why?"

Replying 'overseas adventure, travel and good money', they dedicated the rest of the over-night journey to plying me with beer and making me vow to continue my travels, find real independent adventure – and never, under any circumstance, follow in their footsteps.

Twelve years later Rafa and I were locked in a stare of confusion. Each unsure of what to say to the other. A movement at the door distracted us. The waiter had returned. He held up Rafa's car keys in silence, and like a doctor at a fatality, slowly shook his head.

Raising his arms, Rafa cursed. "*Hijo-de-puta!*"

His arms then falling to his side seemed to pump the last air out of his body. "No. Not my car as well? *Por favor.*"

The waiter shook his head. "All the cars in the car park. Gone."

Rafa slumped onto a bar stool.

Finally, the words came to me. Not about the car, about the Falklands. I realised I could use my line on the market.

"Rafa..."

He looked up as if I'd found his car intact.

I shook my head very slightly. "*...no me gusta* Thatcher."

Rafa paused while the words sank in. Then his desperation was swept away by a smile.

"*Tambien*, and I didn't like Galtieri either." He grinned.

He opened his arms wide.

"You Inglés *loco*. Come here."

I walked towards him, opening my arms to accept his man hug.

On reaching him, he turned his cheek. "*Dame un vaso.*"

The waiter spat his drink out.

The girls yelped with delight.

Yet again, everyone was laughing. I didn't care, I had my friend back. I have never said '*Rapeeedo*' since.

By now we had settled into the market and word was getting around about the lone non-South American artisan. Also, due to Thatcher's war, few British visited, and for many Argentinians I was the first of 'the enemy' they'd met. I was a novelty. The local radio station sent a DJ to the market to interview me.

In carefully spaced words he threw his first question at me. "*Hola. Inglés – como – estas?*"

I understood this as a common greeting, and replied, "Very good. *Muy bien Gracias.*"

He then asked me in Spanish. "Can – I – ask – you – a – question – live – on – the – radio?"

"*Si, Señor.*" I nodded.

The DJ went live and launched into a spiel. He spoke like a football commentator whose team had just entered the penalty box and were inches from scoring a goal. Pausing, the microphone was thrust towards me. I was clueless to what he'd said. The name 'Thatcher' had stood out, and that was it.

Shrugging I answered with the classic phrase for 'I don't understand'.

"*No comprendo.*"

Words gushed from the DJ.

Laughter bounced around the market, leaving me only able to imagine the reaction of the home-audience. I could make out the words. '*Inglés*', '*no comprendo*' and 'Thatcher'. I'd obviously scored some sort of home-goal.

It turned out the DJ had asked me about our ex-prime minister, and on my reply, had told his audience the Englishman didn't understand who Thatcher was.

I fell for his japes three weeks in a row before I refused any more live interviews. My friends on the market begged me to keep 'playing' with him. Although my Spanish was improving, this was a one-sided game. There were only so many balls I could kick in the back of my net. He was a professional who could have eaten me alive in my own language. Besides, I thought he was a right *hijo de puta*.

* * *

Our three-month visas were soon to expire, and our time in Argentina was coming to an end. We planned a small leaving party. It was here, after quite a few drinks, I attempted my first joke in Spanish.

I'd noticed that the hearts of nearly every Latin American bore a lingering natural resentment to the rape and pillage that had happened under the Spanish colonisation. Although there was no excusing the brutality dished out by the Europeans, I'd only just learnt that the Inca themselves had built an empire achieved by rape and pillage. Luciana was of course protective of her Incan heritage. I'd tried to placate her.

"Don't worry, we sent out our bad boys to get even for you. They hung out on Caribbean islands, drinking rum until a Spanish galleon was spotted returning laden with the stolen gold. They'd hoist the Jolly Roger and nick the gold back off the Spanish."

I soon discovered that English pirate jokes didn't go down well with the Incas, Spanish or anyone in Latin American.

There are a few stereotypes in South America. One being that the Argentinians were tight-fisted and hot-tempered. Another being that Colombians are stupid. Jokes were told about them in the same way we tell jokes at the expense of the Irish.

For my first joke in Spanish I thought I'd try a Colombian one that I'd picked up on the market.

It went like this. "A man from Spain," I used my arms to impersonate a plane landing, "In Bogotá."

A Spanish man arrives in Bogotá, I'd got this established.

"He sees a Bogotá *loco* and asks, '*Señor*, where is the cathedral?'"

That got a laugh.

'*Loco*' was a uniquely South American word meaning 'crazy man', used like 'dude' or 'bloke'.

I took the laughter as approval. Gaining confidence, I continued.

"The Bogotá *loco* starts telling him how to get to the cathedral, then suddenly stops and asks, 'By the way, where are you from?'

The Spanish man replies, '*España.*'

'Spain!?' The Bogotá *loco* becomes angry. 'You bastard!'"

I impersonated the Bogotá *loco* knocking the Spanish man to the floor.

"The Spanish man cries, "Señor, why are you beating me?"

The Bogotá *loco* leans over him, 'I know what you did! You Spanish came here. Raped our women. Stole our gold.' He kicks him one more time and spits. 'You *hijo-de-puta*, son-of-a-bitch!'

The Spanish man replies, 'S*i, señor*, but that was five hundred years ago?'

The Bogotá *loco* crosses his arms and says, 'Yes. I know. But I only learnt about it yesterday.'"

Laughter ricocheted around the room. My friends poured my drink high. For once they were laughing with me. I downed my drink in one go.

Rafa turned to me. "Do that impression of the plane landing again."

Still giggling Luciana leant forwards and filled my glass.

"One more time. Show us how the Bogotá *loco* beat the Spanish man."

Luciana must have read my face and added with a gentle smile.

"Don't worry, the joke's funny as well."

The joke is funny?

A crazy coincidence.

What were the chances?

Why this story?

About rape.

About theft.

About violence.

Why Bogotá?

About a tourist who had just arrived?

I tried to calculate if we could lock the doors.

No, the zombie-men were too close.

Besides, the taxi driver's window was already open.

Damn that window.

Then there was the issue of the knife.

'The knife'.

6

KNIVES IN TIME

A KNIFE.

Yes.

I'd seen knives used as threats before. Twice, kind of.

The first time it happened was when walking the back streets of one of the most dangerous parts of Manchester. Hulme in 1989 was famous for drug gangs and gun deaths. Entering an off-licence would involve stepping into a small bullet-proof glass cage that protected the stock and staff from the more exotic customers. The buyer would point at their choice of beer, wine or spirits and the server would take the payment through a bank-like safety-hatch before handing out the goods.

The local graffiti fashion involved mimicking crime scenes. The 'artists' drew the white outline of the slain, decorating the walkways and cat-walks that linked the parts of this once pres-tigious urban project of the 60s. The artwork, although just graffiti, was a chilling reflection of the area's atmosphere as it slumbered in deep decay.

While walking through this rundown estate, late for Hulme's infamous Caribbean Night Club, I passed a gang of young white boys propping up a corner. One of them peeled off from the others and walked beside me. He motioned to something in his pocket. Without thinking, I waved my hand at him – as if at a persistent beggar, and growled. "For Christ's sake, if I had any money, I wouldn't be here, would I?"

Not sure if it was a knife, a gun, or just his hand – I realised I might have done and said the wrong thing. A horrible silence. Ahead of us, I could see the bright lights of a drinking establishment.

Pointing at the pub, I tried to appeal to his logic. "If I had money, at this time of night, I'd be in there, wouldn't I?"

He slowed just slightly. My chance. I accelerated head forward, gritting my teeth, expecting an attack from behind.

The pub was too far to treat as a sanctuary. Needing to get out of his sight so I could run, I acted as if I knew the estate like the back of my hand, and at the next corner took a confident left turn. Straight into a dark cul-de-sac. I could not walk in deeper. I could not walk back out. There was nowhere to go. The dark alley nudged a memory of normal behaviour. I opened my zip and leant against the wall. They'd be with me soon. Unable to relax sufficiently to urinate, I prayed that they would not notice. The gang sauntered by, peered down the alley and walked on. My pose seemed to have worked.

I guess some things are out of bounds.

Well, you'd hope so.

. . .

The second time a knife was used against me, that rule was broken.

While leaning into a pub's urinal, I was grabbed from behind, swivelled and pinned to the wall.

Luciana, a friend Tazmin and myself were visiting a notorious late-night public house called The Blue Jackal in Brixton, London. It was frequented by some of the most colourful and infamous characters of the area. Often coming here once Leicester Square's Imperial Pub was closed, we'd play pool until the early hours.

This evening in particular, I'd gone to the bar to get a round in and on the way had diverted to the gents. Within seconds two guys were pinning me to the wall.

The first guy held a tiny knife to my neck. Barely two inches long. In that moment I learnt that the length of a blade is irrelevant. Two inches of sharpened metal had me at their mercy.

The second guy emptied my pockets.

I knew the landlord and guessed dropping his name would cause them to leave me be within an instant.

"What would Tam say?"

Tam had the broadest smile. His neck appeared thicker than his head. Pure muscle. I'd once seen a gang of three or four try to enter the pub. They'd managed to get partially through the door and with multiple fists flying, the bouncers struggled to push them back. Tam arrived from behind like a bulldozer. He raised his left forearm as a battering ram and ducked his face behind as he pushed forward. With his right arm held high with an empty champagne bottle inside a plastic bag, he pummelled the men's heads like a jackhammer. The bottle bounced off skulls with repetitive dull thuds until it shattered. Not one piece of glass hit the floor, each fragment held within the bag. A bar girl whipped the bag of broken glass out of his hand, while another loaded him up with a new bottle in a fresh bag. Without a pause, to the rhythmic beat of thick glass on thick skulls, the gang were beaten backwards and the pub's main door was bolted shut behind them.

Silence filled the bar. A wave of realisation slowly swept through us, and one by one we grabbed our drinks and moved away from the massive plate-glass windows and took refuge on the inner side of the bar. The traditional frosted glass windows of Britain's public houses offer privacy for those drinking inside, but they also stop people looking out. The windows were expected to become the next port of entry in a shower of glass. They remained intact, the silence was gingerly broken by the odd laugh of relief as we realised the gang had been defeated. I doubt they even knew what hit them.

So, when I said to the muggers, "What would Tam say?" I expected the men to back off.

They just sneered. "This is a black man's pub and you're being taxed."

I had a reply to this one.

"But my girlfriend is black."

Well, she wasn't black, but she was far from white, so I figured I was on safe ground. I sensed a hesitation. They had taken my coins but had not found the tightly rolled notes of my day's jewellery takings, jammed into the finger pocket. I kept talking, hoping to distract them.

I nodded at the coins. "She gave me those to go to the bar

and get her a wine. What am I going to say? When I return with no drink?"

Searching their eyes, I appealed for man to man under-standing.

"She'll kill me."

This was basically true. I'd have some explaining to do. They seemed to sense my fear, working out that once she had dealt with me, they'd be next. The second guy dropped the money back in my pocket.

The guy with the knife pushed my jaw sideways, twisting my neck. "Don't you say a fuckin' word to her."

The other guy smacked me around the head and sneered. "Not to her, and not to Tam."

They pushed me towards the doors. "And if you do? We know you. And you won't see us comin' next time."

Well, I hadn't seen them coming this time. I wasn't going to argue over a minor detail. I left the toilet shaking. I'd just been mugged, or had I?

Were they really more scared of Luciana? Or were they just overwhelmed with man-to-man empathy?

My attempt to return to our table, pretending nothing had happened, failed. Apparently, I was as white as a sheet. Leaving me to nurse my humiliation, with a scream for Tam and the bouncers to follow, Luciana and Tazmin made a beeline for the toilets. I was saved from the further embarrass-ment of having two girls savage my muggers, by a commotion at the door as half a dozen policemen stormed into the pub. They dived straight into the lavatories – beating the girls to it.

The last ten minutes had been surreal. Who had called the police?

Had the muggers taxed someone else shortly before, or had someone seen what was happening to me? We never found out.

The muggers were lucky. The police would let them off more lightly than Tam, and way more lightly than Luciana.

The strangest things happen to me.

Who gets mugged, then has their money given back?

Unheard of.

Impossible.

Surrounded.

Eight men.

With more appearing from the shadows.

Was there a way to escape?

Could the impossible be possible?

It didn't matter.

I'd made a promise.

Never – ever – give up.

IMPOSSIBLY POSSIBLE

WE WERE CROSSING the Andes on a train journey that reached 4,313m – one of the highest railways in the world that is just 1000m less than Everest base camp. As we wound our way through the high passes, navigating past Dallas-style ranches of incredible wealth, that we could only presume had been funded by cocaine production – I realised how critical lungs were for taking in oxygen. In Bolivia, we'd relied on the ancient herbal remedy of tea made from the coca leaf to stave off nausea caused by the altitude. However, now in Peru, with every breath I felt mild claustrophobia.

The train line slowly dropped down to our destination Cusco, a mere 3,400m, or 11,200 feet, above sea level.

Three things struck me immediately about Cusco.

The first was the soldiers in dark black fatigues who lurked with semi-automatics in the back streets, guarding against the Shining Path guerrillas.

The second was the stonework. Ever since I'd spent a year as a dry-stone waller, I'd developed a habit of staring at stone walls, imagining the men who had built them. The making of a dry stone wall is a reverse jigsaw puzzle. The craftsman finds a way of fitting random rocks of various shapes together, placing them in a way to fit as best as possible. No cement is used. The interlocking placement makes the strength of the walls and the resulting patterns reveal the personality of the craftsman – like a signature.

The size of the foundation stones used in the ancient walls of Cusco blew my mind. Many of the blocks would have taken cranes to put in place. The way the stones interlocked was beyond comprehension. The rocks, although seemingly cut, met each other with random faces that nestled together so perfectly, a piece of paper could not be passed between them. A typical household building brick has six sides. A front and a back and four faces that join with the other bricks. Some of the rocks here in Cusco, weighing many tonnes each, had up to fifteen joining faces. The stonework was an enigma. They said these walls had been built by the Incas, a people that had no known written language, of whom Luciana was a direct descendant. Since modern man was unable to replicate this work, the only reasonable conclusion was that the Incas used some sort of technology that we no longer had today.

My puzzled mind had run curious fingers over the stonework chasing the contours. The craft of the stonework was improbable – yet it was there, staring at me proudly from the alleys and walls of the city. The impossibility of the work was undeniably possible.

Thirdly, a painting we'd seen in the local cathedral that day – a huge copy of 'The Last Supper'.

Jesus, as usual, was depicted around the table laden with

the feast with his disciples, however in this version, the artist had adapted the culinary preference to reflect the local cuisine. Taking centre stage of the painting, lying on his back, legs up – lay a whole roasted guinea pig.

My childhood pet guinea pig sprang to mind. After years of love, I'd buried him in our garden with a full funeral, only to discover later that the foxes had dug him up. My pet's 'Last Supper' was a fox's dinner.

Then I thought about the demise of other guinea pigs used in medical experiments. The slow cruel deaths in the name of science. The contrast of fate struck me. The possibility of the irrelevance of a medically supervised death, to a child's love that ends up as a fox's dinner, to another that ends up as the prize dish of the most famous meal of all time – The Last Supper, Cusco version.

That night, within the ancient thick walls of a Cusco pub, though happy-go-lucky with my ten-year-old thirty-a-day habit, I stubbed out my last cigarette. My only assistance was a few hard-boiled candies to sweeten the horror of my mild claustrophobia and struggle to breathe. I stared at that last cigarette in the ashtray, emotionless. Although my beer tasted quite strange, now devoid of the tobacco back-taste that had accompanied every drink for a decade, all I could think about was the impossibility of the interlocking stonework and the guinea pig's life or death lottery.

Yes, Jesus's last meal might have consisted of my childhood pet.

I could be mugged and have the money given back.

I could find my Latin beauty in London, instead of South America.

We could go travelling to earn money, instead of earning to go travelling.

The impossible was possible, which meant the possibilities were endless.

If I could stop smoking dead.

Maybe I might speak Spanish one day?

Even learn to sing?

I might find a way out of this.

Yes, it is looking bad.

We are surrounded.

Nowhere to run.

No time to lock the doors.

The knife – the damned knife.

Remember.

Again.

"Never give up."

Repeat to self.

"The impossible is possible."

2.6 seconds of real time left.

Big, deep, breath.

APPLES, BULLETS AND BEER

AFTER PREVIOUSLY HAVING TRAVELLED through Bolivia, over the high mountain pass to Cusco and onward into Quito Ecuador, we wound our way down from the heights of the Andes to the coastal town of Guayaquil, which had been Luciana's childhood home city.

This was our last major stop before we headed overland into Colombia, where we had flights out of the capital Bogotá, back to Europe.

After a ten-year absence, Luciana was keen to return to El Barrio where she'd grown up. Her aunty Marianna and uncle Miguel, only a few years older than us, gave us a lift in their pickup truck, driving us down the unsurfaced, compressed mud roads that made up El Barrio's grid-like structure. Though poor, space did not seem to be a problem with the houses being separated by gardens and small courtyards, which made it feel like any suburban North American city. However, El Barrio had a reputation.

In silence, Luciana absorbed the form of her old house.

Pointing out a tree in the neighbour's front yard she grinned.

"We used to climb that tree and eat the apples." She nodded towards the house.

"There was a grumpy man who lived there. If he could catch us, he'd beat us with a stick."

At that moment the door of the neighbour's house opened and out came an old man.

"That's him," Luciana whispered.

On seeing Luciana, he walked up to us, his arms wide.

"Is that really you, Isabella?"

A dimple appeared in Luciana's cheek.

"It's Luciana."

"Luciana it is you! I have missed you! Where have you been?"

Turning his attention to me, without taking a breath he continued.

"When she was a little girl," his hand hovered estimating her height as a child, "I used to give her apples. I even let her climb my tree. She loved apples. And her sister did!"

My blank smile diverted his proclamations of his love of Luciana, with Marianna becoming the new recipient.

Luciana leant closer to my ear. "See, when you've been to America, the people that hated you, suddenly love you."

We heard the noise of what sounded like someone cracking a whip.

All of us, except the old man, turned towards the source at the end of the block where some young men were jogging along the transecting road. They could have been a local church's running team, except they wore jeans and T-shirts.

The distant sound again. Three times.

A few of the men, without dropping their momentum – bowed as they ran. A dozen had run by. More appeared. Miguel clapped his hands.

"*Vamos.* Time to go!"

The neighbour, sensing that we were getting away, grabbed both my arms.

"She loved my apples. I fed her every day!"

The sound came again, louder this time. Like two dry sticks being broken.

The young men again bowed briefly as they ran. This time as they rose back up, two of them turned and fired – shooting back at where they had run from.

Everyone was in the pickup except for me. Luciana's old neighbour would not let go.

"She was lovely! My favourite child in El Barrio. Almost like my daughter!"

Mustering the best of my polite smiles, I prised his fingers off my arms. "Yes, she told me all about you too."

As soon as my bum hit the passenger seat, Miguel pushed the accelerator to the floor and the pickup wheel-span away.

Framed by his easy grin, Uncle Miguel explained,

"We need to get back to our house."

"Who is chasing them? The police?" I asked.

"No, just another gang."

He swung the pickup around the next block without touching the brakes. We grabbed onto anything we could to stay upright.

From the back of the truck, Marianna raised her voice, so we'd hear in the front.

"They're running towards our area. Those boys need to

find a place to hide. If they find an empty house and a way in..." She hesitated. "...We need to lock up before they get there."

Miguel beamed at me. "If not, the whole house will be shot up!"

The squeals from Marianna and Luciana filtered into the front. They were enjoying the break-neck ride as if a roller-coaster at a fairground.

We arrived in a cloud of dust, as Miguel brought the pickup to a sliding stop. Within seconds the shutters were brought down on the windows, and all the doors were bolted shut. Even though it was broad daylight, the lights were put on.

A tray of cold beers was slammed on the table by Miguel. With his wide grin, he asked as if there was a choice, "So, what d'ya wanna drink?"

Making ourselves comfortable around the kitchen table, we were soon passing stories like hot potatoes. I tried not to let on that I was listening out for gunshots. With each noise outside I'd look up, making Miguel grin and the girls giggle.

Some photos were slapped on the table by Luciana. They had just been developed and printed.

Marianna started yanking at a photo, "I want the picture of you with Jesus."

"No, it's ours," Luciana protested.

"You can take Jesus home. I keep the photo. You can get another print."

I'd grown my hair past my shoulders, and having not shaved for six months now had a patchy beard. To these crazy Latinas, I looked like the classic Euro-Judean depiction of

Jesus that decorated the Catholic churches. The girls found it highly amusing.

Marianna, taking one picture, pushed another towards Luciana.

"I keep the picture of you and Jesus. You keep the photo of Jesus and the guinea pig."

"Deal," Luciana agreed.

The girls were doubling up with their merriment.

Uncle Miguel met my eye. We cracked fresh beers and slammed the cans together, hard enough that froth bubbled up through the drinking holes.

"*Salud!*"

"Cheers!"

Feeling our distraction, Marianna waved for our attention. "Let me tell you about our taxi ride!"

Miguel nodded to me, "Listen to this one."

Leaning forward, elbows on the table, Marianna launched into her story. "It was a Sunday. Some friends had invited us for a drink. We got ready and caught a taxi."

Miguel, having drunk his beer in one go, burped as he crushed his empty tin in his fist.

"We were at some traffic lights. As the taxi pulls away, these two crazy-men *locos* open our doors."

Eyes wide, Mariana continued. "One *loco* jumps in next to me and the other *muchacho* jumps into the passenger seat."

"Just like that." Miguel clicked his fingers and leant back in his chair.

Marianna flicked a thumb at her husband. "Before he could even open his mouth, the *muchacho* in the front turns around."

Curling his lip like Elvis Presley, Miguel held his hands out, measuring a foot apart. "He's waving a machete at us. This big."

Marianna mimicked him, then opened her hands wider. "This big, or was it this big?"

Miguel slid a new beer towards me.

Attempting to break up the ladies' giggles with a question, I asked, "So what did you do?"

Marianna frowned. "The *loco* tells us to take off our jewellery!"

Miguel nodded, "Yeah. Her gold bracelet and my gold chain. And then, once they had taken that…"

With her eyes wide again, Marianna interrupted. "The *muchacho* tells us to take off our clothes!"

Luciana caught my eye well aware that all our money was buried deep in the secret pocket inside my trousers. She turned back to Marianna. "You still had your underwear on, right?"

"Yes, just my bra and my knickers. He was in his Batman boxers."

Luciana stared at me.

I understood what the look meant. "No, I'm not going to wear underpants. No way."

Marianna screeched, "He doesn't wear any?"

Uncle Miguel flicked the ring pull on his beer until their cackles subsided. He continued. "The driver slows down. The *muchacho* in the front waves his machete and tells me to open the door. The *loco* in the back pushes us both out."

Rolling up her skirt, Marianna showed us the white marks

down her brown legs. "The taxi was still moving. Look. They have healed now."

All hilarity vanished from Luciana's face. "How did you get home?"

"We took a taxi!" Marianna started to smile again. "It was safe. We had nothing left to get stolen."

The girls seemed tickled pink by this.

"But if you two were robbed." She pointed to me. "Trying to catch a taxi naked? You'd both be walking home."

Miguel's eyes met mine. Two men bonded by the wild women of the same family.

Miguel leaned into me. "Do you like football?"

I nodded.

"I've got a spare ticket for the Ecuador Argentina game. Us Ecuadorians gonna show that *loco* Maradona how to play football."

A smile was forming on my face.

"Wanna come?" he asked, knowing full well the answer.

I slammed my beer back into his as an affirmative. Our plans made, we sat in silence watching the girls shriek and howl.

With a scratch that made me cringe, Marianna put an album on the record player and the girls started to dance in almost perfect symmetry – as if a well-practised routine. I'd never seen Luciana dance like this, an X-rated version of her previous dances. To my relief, Miguel, although as fascinated, was also equally ill at ease as me. It struck me how the girls were bonded not only by blood – but by their humour, strength and deep-rooted culture. These women ruled the roost.

When friends in London asked about Luciana, I'd reply with a grin, "She's from Ecuador. I bet you only know of one famous Ecuadorian female and I bet you don't know her name. But you will probably remember her husband. Wayne Bobbit. And if you don't know who he is, I'll let you find out."

"So," Marianna said, sliding a fresh beer to all four of us.

As I gripped the cold beer, she directed her words at me.

"You and Luciana are going to Bogotá?"

I nodded.

"If you think it's bad here, it's way worse there. People don't get pushed out of taxis. People who catch the wrong taxis in Bogotá, vanish."

Her eyes jet black with seriousness.

"They disappear. Just like that."

She clicked her fingers to make her point.

Although I'd just met her, the sudden solemnity seemed strange. She'd always talked with great animation, smiling or laughing.

We all wanted to ask the same question yet remained silent. There was something unspeakable about the vanishings.

Without diverting her eyes from mine, Mariana spoke her Spanish in a gentle slow way, making sure I'd understood each word and its meaning.

"You know what they have to do at the airport now?"

I nodded.

The myth-like stories of Bogotá airport were infamous on the backpacker's grapevine.

She leant forwards, commanding our full attention.

"At the airport. As you leave. They have police checks.

They take the taxi's number plate and the driver's name. They take the name of the passengers and their passport numbers."

It was one thing hearing this story from other travellers. Hearing it from a hardened local brought the warnings to life.

"If someone goes missing…" She sat back in her seat, hands in the air, and beamed.

"They have a record of who did it!"

Luciana was frowning.

"But that's crazy," Luciana poked her aunty's ribs. "Why do the police need to do that? Who would be so stupid to kidnap anyone? In their own car?"

"They're Colombian! Totally *loco*. Even more crazy than us Ecuadorians!"

Their wild, yet warm, laughter from barely a week ago suddenly seemed a million miles away.

'The Colombians are loco.'

I thought the Ecuadorians were loco.

In fact, I thought all South Americans were loco.

And to them, I was the crazy Englishman.

I looked outside our taxi.

Men frozen in time, reaching to open our taxi's doors.

They appeared more like zombies than real men.

Something was missing from their eyes.

I could see it.

I could sense it.

Something had stolen their hearts.

Yet, we are all human.

Knives or no knives.

Right?

LOVE, DRUGS AND SCARS

WHEN EIGHT YEARS OF AGE, Luciana had been playing with a childhood friend when her father had taken her aside, explaining the girl was actually her half-sister. They were just two months apart in age. The news confused Luciana and devastated her mother – yet the family held together.

A few years later, as Luciana played kiss tag with a boy in the neighbourhood, her father stopped the game and again taking her aside, explained that the boy was her half-brother. They were both of the same age.

Shaken, Luciana confided in her mother. This time the family did not hold together. Her mother started to make plans to become independent of the man she'd married and born three children – and started divorce proceedings.

Once done, she left their city and country chasing the North American dream. She promised her children she'd be back for them within three months.

The voyage took her through Colombia, Panama, Costa Rica, Nicaragua, El Salvador and Guatemala to Mexico, where she paid a 'coyote' people smuggler to take her over the border into the USA.

She worked in a New York sweatshop until she owned the coveted green card. This piece of paper allowed her to stay and obtain a legal job, enabling her to finally set up a home – which she did in Puerto Rico. Importantly, the new status of an American citizen extended the right of work and residence to her offspring, enabling her to return to Ecuador for her children – a full three years later.

Luciana and her sister Gabriela, now fourteen and sixteen respectively, were still minors enabling them to join their mother in the States and enter the Puerto Rican education system. Their brother Angel, having just celebrated his eighteenth birthday, was now a few weeks too old and he had to stay behind in the very neighbourhood that his sisters and mother were escaping.

A second cruel twist of fate changed Angel's life forever. When a game of teenage dare escalated, a bottle of wine was stolen and Angel blackened his name on the official records. Due to immigration regulations forbidding immigrants with criminal records, he was forever locked out of North America. Angel had always been a good boy, his mother's deeply loved firstborn, who had done little wrong. But from there on, Angel's life in Guayaquil slowly, and steadily, started to collapse. Those whose wings are denied in the physical outer world, find other ways to fly, and in El Barrio, the price for the momentary freedom of flight, was a just few pesos a hit.

By the time I met Luciana's family ten years later, Gabriela having progressed through the American education system was now a frantically busy high school geography teacher in Florida. The youngest, a trained teacher of dance with her American passport in her back pocket, was travelling around the world as an artisan – with a British boyfriend that called her Luciana.

Meanwhile, back in Guayaquil, Angel acted as a runner of drugs in and out of El Barrio. The rich boys, too nervous to enter the slum, would park on the outskirts and safely order their crack-cocaine from the runners, through their partially opened car windows.

The dealers paid drug addicts like Angel, their commission in the very substance that caused their addiction. This method ensured they came back to work the next day. In turn, this made each awakening to a new day a fresh fight for survival keeping his life balanced on a knife's edge. And in turn, it became impossible for Angel to support his girlfriend and child.

Angel had become trapped in a vortex of bad luck and bad choices. A father who had made three women pregnant at the same time caused his mother to leave. His mother's papers to a new life arriving three weeks too late. A silly teenage dare gone wrong building walls around him. The escapism of drugs. The catch-22 of life as a runner. Angel had become trapped without a means of escape.

These thoughts triggered an awareness of how Luciana and I had really got together. When she'd seen me with the two girls at the bar, it wasn't jealousy that caused her to make up her mind. It was trauma triggered by the parallel situation to her mother finding out she was just one of three women. No wonder Luciana would not let me out of her sight. It wasn't really about me, it was about her father, and she was subconsciously trying to not suffer the same misfortune as her mother. I was witnessing how one man's infidelity set in motion a cascade of events – an avalanche of trauma that swept over the entire family.

When I voiced this, Luciana neither denied nor accepted it. Though when I mentioned her dance with Mariana, she nodded and said, "We were taught to dance like that when we were young girls. The older women told us that if we mastered the dances, we'd be able to hold our men."

With these words, my whole level of understanding shuffled another notch forwards.

We were invited to Luciana's father's for a meal. Angel was also due to be there, which was rare since he'd been banned from the house ever since their father had noticed his visits coincided with vanishing household objects. Still carrying anger for her father, Luciana was reluctant to meet him. With a good dose of my encouragement, alongside the allure of her father and brother in one place, neither of whom she'd seen for nearly half her life – the invitation eventually proved irresistible.

Her father appeared smaller than my imagined image of him. The bright twinkling eyes of this man, who caused three different women to become pregnant at the same time, shined as lively as cats. We swapped pleasantries. However, it was her brother who took our attention.

With a soft, happy grin, Angel sat in front of us, displaying his pleasure to be in the presence of his sister and father – for the first time in his adulthood. With the same eyes, and when content, the same easy charm as Luciana. I felt that I knew him within an instant. Just a year older than me, with his good looks, stubble and reversed baseball cap, he could have been the lead singer of any grunge band. His arms were decorated with intricate and detailed patterns up to his sleeves. These skin designs, that also covered his hands and face, were not created by ink and needle. Every square inch on his visible skin was covered with scars of different shapes and texture, that merged to make abstract, almost paisley-like patterns. Each and every mosquito bite seemed to have scarred him, leaving pitted craters that touched and overlapped like meteor strikes on the surface of the moon. Every injury, however big or small, had left its signature, date and time. Knife cuts were scattered on his arms like a spilt box of matches. The cuts having not been stitched meant the skin grew across the gaps, leaving raised weld-like joins. Not sure if the scarring was caused by a skin disease or by the drugs, I only knew that I'd never seen anything like it before.

Clocking my stares, Angel decided to speak, but his father shot him a warning look.

"My work," Angel muttered with an obedient shrug, silencing my questions before my lips could move. He noticed the angry scar on my right arm, reaching from the inner elbow to near my wrist. He raised his eyebrows, cueing me to talk. A grin appeared on Luciana's face. She enjoyed the variety of scar stories that I used to tease people with. Variations from the vaguely possible to the totally fantastical – from shark attacks to near-death by stampeding giant woodlice. Options were chosen to match people's age, nationality and gullibility.

Bad boys often presumed the scar originated from a knife fight and my silence let their minds paint a story.

My girl's brother deserved only the truth – besides, with his collection of scars, he must have known real life is way crazier than any fiction. I sat back and growled.

"Dodgy surgeon. Hungover and bored on a Sunday morning."

The words caught his attention.

"I bust the radius bone clean in two, falling off a fence. It made the same noise as if I'd broken a branch over my knee."

He winced.

"The surgeon bolted the bones back together. Couldn't be bothered to do the job properly. Ninety degrees off."

Demonstrating the point visually, I placed the tips of my thumbs together, nails aligned – and then twisted one thumb by a quarter of a rotation.

I showed him the lack of movement in my arm by swivelling my wrist. "Can't get my hand flat to accept money, or even type."

Luciana nudged him and whispered. "Or wipe his arse."

Waving my left hand in the air I added, "Luckily, I still have this one to help me out."

Angel beamed ear to ear, with the same smile that had caused me to succumb to his sister.

The warmth between us made Luciana happy. Every time I became stuck for a word, probably nervous that I'd embarrass her in front of her male family by standing up and re-enacting scenes, she translated for me.

Angel reached to lift his T-shirt. His father leant forward to try to stop him but was too late.

Most sisters would have cried with what we saw. Maybe Luciana had used up all her tears in her early years, while waiting for her mother. She barely flinched, visibly at least.

Her father slumped back into his seat.

Although the skin under Angel's shirt was not pock-marked to the extent of his arms and face, a huge thick zip-like scar ran over an indented hollow that seemed as if someone had stolen a small handful of his flesh.

"This one," Angel said, "made by a surgeon too. Where he cut a bullet out."

His eyes followed mine to a wild psychedelic pattern that looked like a cross between an exploding firework and a poorly made spider's web.

"That one?" he said, reading my mind. "Stabbed with a bottle."

He mimed the process – a flick of the wrist, smashing the bottom half off – then a quick stabbing motion.

His father shuffled in his chair, stood up and offered the juice carton to us. With a better view of Angel, he paused mid-air as if he was looking at his son's body for the first time.

Angel rested his fingers on another starburst.

"This one. Another bottle."

His fingers danced over the scars as if leading me around a city on a map.

"Knife. I was slashed." He pointed to another long thin scar. "And that one."

"This one? Bottled again."

He pointed at some short but wide scars.

"Knife, stabbed. Here and here. And this one, a bullet. Went straight through."

How was he still alive? Surely each stab wound or bullet should have killed him?

His body was a picture book, depicting the attempts on the life of a man who refused to die.

Swivelling on his chair he turned and pulled the T-shirt over the rear of his head. "See this?"

The scars on his back, although fewer, were deeper and aggressive looking. Three more bullet marks. The one that grabbed our attention intersected with another long zip-like scar that ran down his spine.

"That long one. A surgeon tried to take out the last bullet. They gave up. Thought I was gonna die anyway." Jabbing his thumb towards a point on his spine he could not reach, he added, "Press there, between the ribs. You can feel the bullet."

Luciana shot me a glance, letting me know not to move an inch.

From the corner of his eye, Angel also caught the warning and he sat back down grinning – his eyes locked again on mine. He flicked his head over his shoulder, refer-ring to the bullet scars on his back. "I got them climbing a fence too."

He grinned slyly, looking at my scar.

"To the *Hijo-de-puta*, son-of-a-bitch, fuck-it-up surgeons."

He leant forward, tapped my glass of juice with a loud chink, and sat back in his seat. In my mind's eye, Angel had shrunk the scar on my arm, to have the significance of a mere scratch.

The three of us looked to his father, who still held the carton of fruit juice mid-air ready to serve us. He seemed to have his jaw stuck, his mouth half open.

"What?" Angel asked him, shrugging his shoulders with mock innocence.

No-one knew how Angel had collected all the other scars. But everyone knew about the bullet holes on his back. A court case and a time spent in jail was public knowledge. Angel had been caught red-handed burgling a house. As the police arrived at the front, he'd run out of the rear. As he was scrambled up the tall perimeter fence to escape, the police shot him three times in the back. Two bullets had been removed but the last bullet had become wedged by his spine. The doctors warned that it might shift, and cause paralysis at any time.

His mother saved the $1,500 needed for the operation so that, once he was out of jail, he could have the bullet removed. The money was duly sent and duly vanished. The family presumed he'd spent it feeding his addiction, though at the time the various stories bandied around of dangerous debts and intrigue, confused them.

A year later, his mother had again saved the money needed for his operation. After many a phone call and promise of reform, she sent it. This time, he filled the fridge with food and bought a present for the mother of his child and the rest of the money vanished – the bullet remaining wedged near his spine.

His two sisters had now forbidden their mother from sending any more money.

Angel asked Luciana for some money for his child. Luciana, ruthless with her tough love, would not give him a dollar. Weaker, I slipped him a couple of notes.

I had one head start on Angel; sharing his sister's eyes, I could read him like a book. With Luciana out of earshot, he confided in me that his mother still sneaked payments to him.

He told me because he wanted me to know that whatever a disaster he might have become – however much he'd messed up his life, and the lives of those close to him – that someone still loved him unconditionally, irrespective of his addictions, cheating, theft and lies. Although his mother had left him behind, their bond of mother-son lived on. He needed me to reflect and confirm this.

I didn't need to pretend. On meeting their mother I'd sensed her profound love, as well as her deep guilt and helplessness. The 'three-weeks-too-late scenario' had haunted her.

By the time I'd met Luciana's mother, she was happily remarried and living in Florida and had adopted four boys from New York care homes. Not just any kids, she'd taken under her wing the children of crack addicts. 'Crack babies' as they were called.

Thinking I had a bit of a knack with animals and kids, nearly always able to get the hardest, most challenging, tantrum-prone child to smile – the boys didn't faze me. Three of them were healthy, and although troublesome, manageable. Lovely and lively children who, having been deprived of stimulus in their early years simply craved attention more than most. In the short time we knew each other, we became firm friends.

However, the fourth and youngest of her adopted children scared me. He had a wild fury in his eyes. His mother had been a helpless crack-head while pregnant. Although now four years old, he soiled his pants hourly as he writhed in pain, arching his back as if something was trying to escape from within him. His deep inner rage, clearly visible in his eyes, unnerved me. I couldn't find a connection. The doctors had explained that he might not live to be a teenager. She stayed up with him, night after night, trying to soothe his inner torment as he lashed out striking anyone near. There were no boundaries to Luciana's mother's resilience. She loved that boy beyond the possible. Truly one of the bravest, devoted and loving women I'd ever met.

And right now.

Her youngest daughter was with me.

In the back seat of the wrong taxi.

In the wrong part of town.

In the wrong city.

At the wrong time of night.

And I was responsible.

It was my fault.

I had assured Luciana's mother that her daughter would be safe with me.

The knife moved again.

Just a frame.

2.4 seconds of real time left.

10

BOGOTÁ – A FATAL MISTAKE

AFTER BUYING our leather presents in the Ecuadorian border town, we crossed the frontier into Colombia. Running out of time to catch our flight home, we jumped on a small propeller-powered plane for a short and noisy internal flight to Bogotá. As we cut through Colombia's night skies we barely had the chance to admire the street lights, mapping the presence of passing towns below, before starting our descent into Bogotá.

By the time we landed, the sensible people were tucked up in bed and asleep. This was the graveyard shift. Since we'd caught an internal flight there were no customs to clear and we walked directly from the runway into the main part of the airport, with as little fuss as if we'd caught a bus.

It was one o'clock in the morning and the handful of other passengers seemed to have melted into thin air. The airport became eerily quiet. The shutters had already been pulled down on the exchange booths, shops and boutiques. Everything seemed to be closed. A few bored cleaners pushed big brooms across the floor. Drawn towards the exit sign, I ditched our trolley and while stifling a yawn, hoisted a rucksack onto each shoulder, letting Luciana take the day bags.

We ventured out into the night air and soon found a line of yellow Bogotá taxis, bathed in the orange glow of the sodium street lamps. No queue existed. We seemed to be the only passengers in sight. Some taxi drivers lay across their front seats, fast asleep. Leaning against a lamp post, a couple of drivers drew on cigarettes as they silently weighed us up, taking in each part of us from head to toe. They reminded me of vultures.

Searching down the line of cars, I found a better option. A taxi with not only the taxi driver asleep across the front seat, but a uniformed police-officer asleep across the rear seat.

Relieved, I chose this taxi.

The driver, still rubbing the sleep from his eyes, helped us place our bags in the car's boot. Luciana was soon comfortable on the rear seat with our small carry-on bags, while I sat in the front alongside the driver.

I looked outside, wondering where the policeman had gone.

He had vanished into thin air.

We'd barely arrived.

And I'd made a major mistake.

I knew better.

Much better.

I knew all about the police.

LOSING MY RELIGION

WE'D STARTED to hear stories about the real dangers of South America as soon as we arrived in Argentina. Comparatively recently, blacked-out Falcon cars had turned up in the dead of night to 'arrest' victims from their homes. Like a faceless mafia gang, these vehicles also cruised the streets in broad daylight. Car doors would be flung open and people dragged inside, never to be seen again.

I asked an Argentinian friend if he'd witnessed anything.

His reply came with a helpless shrug of the shoulders. "Even when our neighbours were snatched. Sometimes friends that we'd grown up with since childhood. We presumed they must have done something wrong. So we said nothing. We minded our own business and accepted it."

Pinochet, in neighbouring Chile, having played the same game was thought to have murdered at least three thousand in his country. A Hollywood movie called *The Missing* based around North American passport holders caught up in these events, documented the deeds. The perpetrators still held power over the media and courts and remained free men. Pinochet kept close friends in high places, who protected him on the international scene. The ex-British prime minister, who started the Falkland War to improve her popularity ratings – Margaret Thatcher – was one of his excusers.

Thousands of Argentinians, who dared have opinions and thoughts contrary to the US-backed Neo-liberal regime, disappeared during these times. Most of those kidnapped were students or left-wing activists deemed a danger to the military junta. The government wiped the names of these people from official records, with the logic that people who had never existed, could not vanish and therefore the women claiming to have lost children were obviously mad. The authorities called these ladies *Las Locas*, or 'The crazy ladies'. In the absence of state help, the mothers joined forces to create their own database of the missing, by simply recording how many of them had lost their offspring. The figure they arrived at was over thirty thousand. Two competing 'truths' wrestled for a place in the history books: the government's truth versus the mothers' truth.

The government soon realised they were losing this information war, and resorted to kidnapping and murdering some of the mothers. It made no difference. The mothers' love for their lost children was a force they could not defeat. By the time of our visit in 1994, these women had been holding a vigil in the Plaza de Mayo – demanding state recognition of their losses – that had now lasted seventeen years. The *Madres de Plaza de Mayo* never gave up.

The whispered rumour behind closed doors was that many of 'The Disappeared' had been flown far out to sea in military aeroplanes – and pushed out.

I'd doubted this possibility and quoted the maxim that the sea never held secrets; that the bodies would have been washed up and found. The looks I received were enough to realise that I'd been told the truth. Dirty secrets from a dirty war that no-one wanted to remember – or, let me know how they knew.

By 1994, although the governments had changed, the walls of Argentina were stained by shadows of the past. The killers still held power, wearing new guises. The *Madres de Plaza de Mayo* were still protesting weekly, and every café I visited had a collecting box on the counter for the young conscripts disabled in *La Guerra Malvinas*. Coming from a country with more skeletons in the closet than Jack the Ripper, Argentina could not be judged for her politics or past. I adored the people's love of life, humour and warmth and I soon formed deep friendships. Loving the great outdoors, the land itself was awe-inspiring with her variety of unspoilt natural landscapes, from the frozen tip of Tierra de Fuego to the northern humid jungle or mountainous borders. A land populated by wild cats, and prairies where the cowboys or Los Gauchos, roamed with herds of free-range cows. With an abundance of beef, each Argentine man, woman and child infamously ate a record-breaking ninety kilos of meat a year. The Argentine a*ssado* barbecues tasted second to none. While the antibiotic, hormone-laden, burgers and steaks of North America were creating an obesity epidemic, the carnivorous

Argentinians were some of the healthiest people I'd seen worldwide. To top it all off, the women shone with dream-like auras, and the wine was divine. Argentina rose to the pinnacle of my ideal countries and at twenty-seven years old, given half a chance, I would have emigrated on the spot.

The only country that held higher possibilities was Colombia with five climate zones, including the Amazonian tropical rainforests, savannah, steppes, deserts and the Andean mountain climate. Not forgetting the country bordered two coasts, the Pacific and the Caribbean. Colombia was over-flowing with possibility. Although the country was infamous for the production of cocaine, the FARC liberation army and the highest murder rate in the world – the people themselves had a terrific reputation. I'd already formed fantasies of buying some land on the coast and whiling my later years away in a hammock to the laughter of grandchildren. Colombia would be our last stop and I could barely wait.

Our travels took us towards Brazil and the stunning Foz do Iguacu. These magical waterfalls mark the meeting point of three countries, Paraguay, Argentina and Brazil where the blood red waters tumble over a massive U-shaped canyon. At twice the height of Niagara, and three times the volume, the sight of these waters, that fell in shades from deep red through to white, were unforgettable. Luciana and I were hypnotised, and spent two full days getting drenched in the spray as we sampled the falls from each country's viewpoint. A natural wonder of the world.

From here we moved on into Brazil, where we started to hear of a new horror story. Rumours of dark deeds that were not historical, but contemporary.

Some artisan friends, who we'd met in the market in Argentina, hosted us deep in the suburbs of São Paulo. From here, we caught the suburban train daily into the heart of the city and sell our jewellery in the main square Praca de Republica. The park sat as a rare patch of green in a grey sea of tall buildings, crisscrossed by busy roads.

Massive inflation had been slaughtering the Brazilian economy. The face value of the currency halved in value every month. As soon as anyone possessed cash, it needed to be spent or traded for a stable hard currency. Instead of changing my jewellery prices daily, I priced the rings with the letters A-F. Each morning I'd visit the exchange booths and set up the chart according to the day's rate. When customers asked what price a 'D' was, I'd refer them to the list. One day that might have meant paying two hundred thousand cruzeiros, the next day it might be two hundred and twenty-two thousand cruzeiros. The inflation confused all of us –the sellers, the customers and the locals – but with this system, the customer always paid the same actual price relative to hard currency. The bigger businesses seemed to not be so agile. They'd only change their prices once every few weeks. I watched one music chain store closely. A compact disc that might have been fifteen dollars in the States or Europe, would briefly be priced at the equivalent of twenty-five dollars. As the currency deflated day by day, the real dollar price would drop like a stone.

Within a few days, the album would be the equivalent of

fifteen dollars, and then, I'd wait until the last moment before the next price rise and snap them up for five dollars. The following day the store would reset their prices, with the music again costing the equivalent of twenty-five dollars before the repeated nosedive. It was here in Sao Paulo, being a slow convert, that I bought my first Nirvana albums.

The money itself had been printed with three smaller zeros after the main number that were greyed out with a diagonal line – in preparation for the day, when the zeros were simply no longer used. Already, instead of saying fifty thousand, we'd just say fifty – and people understood.

The financial mayhem was topped off by an incredible sight. The paper bin of a café's toilet, full of bank notes used as toilet paper. Once back at my jewellery stand, I did a few calculations that confirmed the low-value note was comparable in value to a single sheet of toilet paper. The previous user of the café's lavatory had not wasted his money.

My customers warned me, time after time, that I'd be mugged for the small box of silver jewellery. However, having blended in with the others that worked the street, I sensed my back was covered.

One young lad with deformed legs, who pushed himself around on a homemade skateboard-like contraption, became my silent soul-mate. Although neither of us spoke the other's language, we were tuned in to the same wavelength. With winks, grins and raised eyebrows we found the same things funny and shared a similar appreciation of female beauty.

Each late afternoon, as all street sellers packed up and left the Praca de Republica, I'd hoist my friend and his board up, balancing him on my shoulder. Although probably in his early twenties, due to his small deformed leg bones, he only had the weight of a child. We'd then run down the steps, laughing as we passed through the train's ticket barriers without paying. Once on the train, I'd lift him down and he'd pull himself through the carriages selling gum and little cardboard packs of juice. This became our routine.

Our new Brazilian friends included a variety of sellers, buskers and beggars, and it was through these people that we first heard rumours of the street children being murdered.

How could this even be possible? Not a word was mentioned within the newspapers. Not a sound bite about it on the radio, or television. Surely, the murder of any children, on any scale, would make international headlines?

I heard the stories again and again, and slowly and surely, the ugly truth was finding its way, crawling and hiding, under my skin. The possibility, that in deed, the children were being killed by the police.

From São Paulo we took a long bus journey, away from the mayhem of the big city, up the coast to a quiet little seaside resort north of Bahia, called Clareza do Sol. A town famous for extraordinary juice stalls and stunning beaches that was also the heart of Capoeira dance.

The locals explained that the dance derived from the time of slaves in chains. With only their legs free, the slaves developed a form of self-defence that involved kicking and ducking with the grace of dance movements. A hybrid of martial arts and dance, that Luciana wished to add to her repertoire.

Each day, once the heat of the sun's rays had passed,

wooden carts would line the town's high street, piled high with tropical fruits cut into the most amazing patterns and structures – a tourist sight in its own right. Any fruit juice that could be imagined would be conjured up. Once night fell, rum or vodka might be added, or for a little extra kick, a locally grown ingredient called guarana. Having not heard of it before, the lady assured us that once consumed, we'd dance all night. I ordered one each for Luciana and me. The taste of the brown powder hidden in the juice, obscured by the rum made an easy drink. We ordered another, before heading to our favourite open-air beachside club and thought we were still on our first dance when the sun rose.

We joined ranks with these seaside juice stalls and set up our jewellery table. We felt very lucky as we now sold our handicrafts to rich tourists from Sao Paulo and Rio, enabling us to earn their city money, whilst avoiding the city fumes and urban crime.

Full of good intentions to learn the language, I dug out my original Spanish word list and added the Portuguese words.

Si – Yes – *Sim*

Non – No – *Não*

Que – What – *O que*

*Por favou*r – Please – *Por favor*

Gracias – Thank you – *Obrigado*

Señor – Mister – *Senhor*

Señora – Mrs – *Senhora*

Gringo – Foreigner – *Estrangeiro*

Vino – Wine – *Vinho*

The Portuguese words were similar enough to Spanish. I tried to speak a few but ended up with sentences half in

Spanish and half in Portuguese. As we were soon to head back into Spanish speaking Latin America, I figured I was best off sticking with one language and learnt a few words like *Obrigado* for thank you, and spoke everything else in Spanish. Strangely, the Brazilians seemed to understand me even better than the Argentinians. Either that, or it was my body language that was becoming clearer.

It was here on the market, whilst we let the hours drift by as we waited for customers, that we had time to talk and think. A good friend Jorge ran our neighbouring stall – a well-built, tall Brazilian who funded his worldwide travels by selling handmade leather bracelets. Obsessed with doing hardcore detoxes, he'd use them to lose kilos whilst turning his complexion from a sickly grey to a rosy pink. His logic being that once his body became clean and healthy, he'd earned the licence to eat endless junk food. Once the grey complexion returned and he'd piled on the pounds, he'd make preparations for the next detox. He'd discovered the diet regime whilst reading about a small group of prostitutes working in the favelas of Rio who had astonished health workers by not using protection, yet remaining HIV free. Their secret being a monthly juice detox. Once detoxified, their unburdened immune system could easily fend off the feared virus. Jorge used the knowledge to keep himself disease free, and certain North American burger chains in business.

He was also fascinated by the miniature full keyboard of my folding Psion pocket computer that had been Britain's must-have Christmas present of 1993. With 512kb of memory and 2mb of RAM, it amazed us that we could hold a computer in the palm of our hands with more power than the computer that sent man to the moon. It held a wonderful new application called a spreadsheet which again blew us away and we spent hours learning to program the cells to record sales and calculate our stock buying. We toyed with the radical idea that portable compact disc players would soon be a thing of the past once flash discs became cheap and music would be played on contraptions, free of moving parts. We were excited to think that these appliances would soon have colour screens, though it was hard to imagine. And whilst we owned a device to play games on, another to play music on, a further device to use as a word processor or spreadsheet, yet another to tune into the radio and not forgetting another to take pictures with – we toyed with the idea, that not too far into the future, we'd carry a single device that did everything.

It was mid-April on the day after the Easter weekend, and Cobain's recent death filled the newspapers. I checked myself in the mirror for any signs that the age of twenty-seven might surprise me with sudden suicidal thoughts. I couldn't detect a thing. In fact, living and working in the Latin lands of my dreams, I was as excited about life as I'd ever been.

During the evening chats with Jorge, fifteen years my senior, I voiced my confusion over Kurt Cobain. If I wasn't suicidal at twenty-seven, why was he? With millions of fans, zillions in the bank, filled with creativity and unfinished projects surely he felt as excited by the tomorrow as me? And, most of all, with a child in tow – why would he kill himself?

We knew plenty of people messing around with heroin. Not one was suicidal. In fact, heroin was their medicine that stopped them caring about anything enough to become suicidal. Cobain was known for the song title 'Nevermind', not 'I Can't Go On – I'm giving up'.

The reports said that Cobain had injected himself with three times more heroin than required to cause death. If used intravenously, a substance enters the bloodstream reaching vital organs within seconds. Surely he would have lapsed into immediate unconsciousness and the needle would have been found hanging from his arm?

However, apparently after injecting the lethal dose he had carefully folded his drug-taking paraphernalia away, before proceeding to shoot himself.

Heroin users gauge their 'medicine' so as not to overdose and accidentally kill themselves. If a user wanted to commit suicide, the dose to make a clean and successful job of it was at hand. Easy to slip away, leaving things as tidy as possible for the family. He knew what he was doing. Why the need to blow half their head off?

We tried to imagine how difficult it was to place a long shotgun in your mouth whilst lying on your back. How do you reach for the trigger? Tricky. But surely nigh on impossible once a massive heroin overdose had already caused unconsciousness or death? Begging the question, how can anyone kill themselves twice?

This led us to think about another rock-legend who also hadn't made it past twenty-seven. Hendrix's story conjured up more questions. The autopsy stated wine had been found in his lungs. How did he drown on red wine, when he barely drank? Was he that out of practice he'd forgotten how to breathe and swallow at separate times?

I'd breathed in water once. On dry land. I told Jorge the story.

Whilst in Hong Kong in the corridor of our 11th storey hostel, I'd been drinking from a bottle of water, when someone cracked a joke I wasn't ready for. I laughed and breathed in some water. I ran into the toilet banging my back. No luck. After what felt like an age, I ran back out to my friends gesticulating for help – blue in the face. One of them was not only a trained paramedic but a very tall and strong member of the Dutch international basketball squad. My six foot two frame was an easy lift for him. Grabbing me from behind, he picked me up and slammed me down, using his grasp to pump my rib cage as my feet hit the floor. I coughed up half an egg cup of water. He'd given me the Heimlich manoeuvre. Giggling with the shock, I marvelled at how such little water had rendered me incapable of breathing.

If Hendrix was alone, who had made him laugh and breathe in the wine? Our minds span as we searched for answers. If he'd choked, why hadn't he run outside to get help? Hendrix had been found with his hair and clothing soaked in red wine. His stomach was also full of the red liquid, yet there was almost no alcohol in his blood. This meant he died before he could absorb the alcohol or feel even slightly drunk. Who would buy a good red and pour it over themselves? And whilst still sober? I'd met some wild people and spent a lot of time with hardened drinkers – yet I had never seen, or heard of anything similar.

Although fascinated by these apparently assisted-deaths, a slight sense of self-centred relief overcame me. It turned out that being twenty-seven was not booby-trapped by some age-related trigger designed to snuff out wanna-be rock stars. Maybe, after all, I was safe.

Meanwhile, while selling bracelets and solving distant murder cases, we were completely and utterly oblivious to the real intrigue of the town. Something, occurring in plain sight right under our noses.

Even though our pension owned a fantastic setting, not only facing the sea but near the central fruit juice market – the only guests were ourselves. My simple mistake had been to link the lack of guests, to the plentiful leaks. The place must have been missing half its roof tiles. Even though we took the room with the least drips, we still needed to position our bed centrally and set at a diagonal, to avoid the multiple rivulets of cascading water that appeared with each rainfall. Hence it was no surprise that no other guests existed. The place, being close to our work, cheap and well fortified with countless door bolts meant the benefits outweighed the inconveniences.

The pension manager, lacking the distraction of other guests, was keen to talk, but we were always busy, either making stock, selling or heading out to the beach or clubs. He upped the stakes offering us drinks and eventually we accepted. Over a cold beer one evening, he dropped into the conversation that his job at the hotel was temporary. His real job was in Rio and he was only temporarily up here on the coast.

Obliged into conversational politeness by the beer I'd accepted, I asked, "What is your real job then?"

"I'm a policeman," he grinned.

Great. Luciana caught my eye and raised her eyebrows.

Leaks were one thing. Living with one from the other side pushed her limit.

I widened my eyes just slightly, letting her know my thoughts in an instant. "Yes. There are leaks. Yes, this place is a hole. But it is close to the market, and it's me that has to carry the table, and bags each night. And we just accepted his drinks. Be nice."

She slumped back in her chair.

Still halfway through one of his beers, I continued the small talk.

"So why did you take a sabbatical?" I imagined the answer being work-related stress or something.

"They're pleased with me. The sabbatical is my reward."

"Who is pleased with you?'

"My bosses in Rio."

"The chief of police?"

"Yes."

This was a reverse interrogation, where he was shepherding me to ask the next question.

"Why are they so pleased with you?"

He grinned. "They had a bounty on two men."

A 'Wanted Dead or Alive' poster from a western filled my mind.

"You mean like a bounty to catch them?"

"Yes," he smirked.

He held up two fingers like a gun and blew imaginary smoke from the nozzle.

Although a worn thirty-something-year-old, he was small, with a scrawny frame and baby-like features. As if a fifteen-year-old, his beard had grown in fluffy patches. There was an air of nervousness about him that I associated with deceit. His eyes darted around the room. He fidgeted with his beer can, cigarettes, or whatever he was holding.

I continued. "What had the guys done? The ones you were looking for?"

He shrugged. "Some gangsters. They were on the run. They had gone up to the far north-west near the Amazon. All outlaws run there. It's Brazil's wild-west. People can make themselves disappear."

This time I remained silent.

Giving up the wait for me to prompt him, he continued.

"So I followed them."

Turning slightly away from me he succeeded in hiding his eyes, but his smile gave his child-like excitement away.

"So, when you found them, what happened?"

He laughed and turned back to me. "Yeah. I found them. In this small town. Followed them until we came to a foot-bridge. I knew this was a good place."

I was getting into the swing of this. He couldn't just tell me the story, he needed me to pull the story out of him like a thorn.

"Why was the footbridge a good place?"

"You see. They could only move in two directions. Away from me. And towards me. But not sideways. Made it easy."

I imagined an old western. The sheriff making a stand against the outlaws. Clint Eastwood narrowing his eyes, chewing on his tobacco, giving them one last chance to turn themselves in.

"What did you do? Say, you're under arrest?"

He laughed, shaking his head as if he'd heard a good joke.

"They had a bounty on their heads."

This time he wasn't waiting for me to ask the next question. "I just walked up behind them."

Again, using two fingers to form a gun. He lifted his hand. His demeanour changed. His mind no longer in the pension. He'd gone back in time, to the moment.

He tilted the gun sideways. Bit his bottom lip. Eyes squinting. A mad yet determined anger.

He fired his gun.

"BUFF!"

Moving his aim slightly.

"BUFF!"

He lowered his eyes with mock humility.

"I shot them both in the back of the head. One bullet each. Didn't need any more."

His cheeks grew colour blushing under his own self-praise. The re-enactment seemed to have quenched an inner thirst, bringing him peace and halting his fidgeting.

He looked back up at me.

"Yeah, they were so pleased with me in Rio, they've given me six months off."

Then added sheepishly. "Fully paid."

As if waking from a dream, realising where he was, his face lit up as he spread his arms wide – taking in the pension.

"And now – here I am!"

Not one person was able to visit Brazil without becoming immediately aware of the volume of children living on the street. The bigger the city, the more the children. Our small seaside town of Clareza do Sol kept about a hundred and fifty sleeping in the open air under the street lights by the beach.

Children from barely four or five years old, all the way through to more mature teenagers. The older children looked after the younger ones. All had been abandoned or orphaned. Without parents, family or state benefits, the kids survived by their wits, theft or even prostitution. Money meant food, and food meant staying alive.

The stories from Sao Paulo still reverberated. Could it be possible that these street-kids were culled like wild dogs? I now had access to a man who would know the truth. The chance to ask him finally arose one night when, again over a beer, he told us a story.

"Five of us went into the favela to arrest this *micróbio*. The guy's not been paying his bills. He's surprised to see us. Reaches for a drawer. Me and my partner. We fill him with holes."

"Why did you do that?"

The manager pulled a face at my stupidity and sneered. "The drawer."

"What was in the drawer?"

"A gun. But when we looked. It was full of cash. The dumb fucker was gonna pay us. Should have said something."

He shrugged, leant back and placed his hands behind his head.

"See. Life is tough in Rio."

"Yeah." I nodded, thinking about what the man had been thinking as they fired. "Life is really tough."

The manager nodded with a smile as If I'd said it first.

This was my moment to ask.

"What about the street-kids?"

He looked at me in silence.

I chipped in as casually as I could. "I mean, do you have problems with them?"

"Dangerous."

I frowned as if I didn't understand.

Challenged, he took the bait.

"Those kids are lethal. The young ones especially. The older ones. Once they are about ten. They see us and squeal like pigs."

He waved his hands in the air, impersonating a child using a high-pitched voice.

"Don't shoot, Mister Cop. I've done nothing. Honest."

He spat on the floor. "They throw their weapons to the floor. They even piss themselves."

Keeping a blank face I nudged him further. "So, if they are that frightened, what do you do?"

He grinned. "If they look really scared. I mean if they're shitting in their pants, I don't shoot. Otherwise..." He looked me in the eye and rocked his jaw side to side.

"What about the younger ones, then?"

He snapped. "I don't think. I just fucking shoot them."

I recoiled at his words and his anger.

He didn't like my reaction and jumped out of his seat.

"They come to you like this."

He swaggered towards me swinging his arms and rocking his hips – a huge smile on his face.

"Hey, Mister Cop... how are you? How's your girlfriend?"

He grabbed an imaginary gun and ran at me, firing into my face.

Now leaning over me, my back bent over the chair, he

breathed sweaty hot air on my face. He held the pose for a second too long, before laughing and standing back.

"See the young ones have no fear. They're not scared of anything. Too young to fear us cops. Too young to fear death." He sat back in his chair.

"See? That's why. When I see the young ones." He grinned at us happily. "I shoot them. Before they shoot me."

Luciana broke the silence.

"But how do you know if they have a gun? They are just kids."

He sneered. "Look. My partner was killed by a street-rat. He was thinking like you, 'Just a kid.' Nice cops don't live long."

He said 'nice' as if the word was disease ridden.

I took a swig of beer. It tasted foul. I tried reasoning with him, "The kids can't all have guns. I've seen them. Most are begging or selling stuff."

Seemingly more respectful of my European ignorance, he replied slowly and calmly. "Look. There was this old lady in Rio. Just like you guys. Nice. She feels sorry for this one kid. Takes him home. Looks after him. Like her own son. Was like that for months. Then one day she comes back to the house. Everything gone. The mouse had let the others rats in. They had cleaned her out. Eighty years old. Nothing left. See? Once they are on the street, they can't go back."

I dared to ask the big one. "How do you feel then?"

He raised a questioning eyebrow.

"I mean, when you kill a child?"

Turning his eyes away from me, he held a hand to his belly, his face contorting just a little.

"The first time, I was nearly sick."

His mouth curled back in disgust. "But then, after you've killed a few, it's easy."

Taking his hand off his belly, he looked me in the eye to make his point.

"Just like killing cockroaches. You don't feel a thing."

Taking a large glug from his beer, he belched, then leant forward resting his elbows on his knees – with the stance of a mother lecturing a child.

"Look. These kids. Once in the gutter, they are always in the gutter. They are vermin. Best off dead. And someone has to do it."

A few days later, still digesting what we'd heard, someone else came to stay at the pension. An Austrian lady introduced not only as the partner of the pension manager but also the owner. Blond hair, blue eyed and well dressed. With her black frame glasses, straight chin-length hair, she came across like a librarian on holiday. However, she clearly wore the trousers and watching the manager dance to her tune, amused us. Glad to shake off his fantasies of vigilante justice, as the products of a bored man with an overactive imagination, the air inside the pension suddenly became lighter to breathe.

To welcome the owner back, a seafood barbecue was organised, and we were roped in to help with the preparation. The kitchen was cleaned. Fish, prawns and a bucket of large live crabs were bought – and whilst the ladies made the salad – the two of us men were sent out to buy missing vegetables.

This was not only the first time I had spoken to the manager in daylight hours, but it was also the first time I'd been outside of the hotel with him.

As we chatted, walking down the sea road, a strange thing started to happen. The street kids hanging around the street lights, half asleep or sitting in small circles, stood up and started to move away from us. As we made progress down the seafront, the next group rose to their feet and started jogging away. Not one of the children let us within fifty metres. We were causing a wave of fear to run through them as if pigeons taking flight to avoid a dog. And all without a sound. Once we were at a safe distance, they settled down again, taking up the same positions, casually, as if nothing had happened.

Their movement and action reminded me of the fly-pitchers of London's Leicester Square.

Two young boys stopped and turned to look back. Only then did I realise the other kids had moved without making eye contact. These boys were looking directly at us.

The manager's eyes glowed. He held up his two-finger pistol, took aim at the boys and fired. This time the show being for them. They turned and jogged to increase the distance between us. With a self-satisfied smirk, the manager checked to see if I'd caught what he'd done, before he slotted his imaginary gun back in the rear of his belt with a grin.

How could a man take pleasure in scaring these kids? His actions confirmed that all of this rubbish about guns and children could not be real. A weak man, chuffed that some poor kids and idiot tourists had fallen for his tough-man yarns.

Thinking about similar stories, yarns and myths I calmed a little.

I thought about how the Scots tease American tourists with the myth of haggis hunting. Although meatballs can't fly, people believe what they're told and go hunting for them.

The Australians tease tourists with the warnings of Drop Bears. Stories of small yet aggressive bears that drop from trees gouging out the eyes of the unlucky. On my first week in Sydney, whilst walking by a riverside, a known traditional Drop Bear habitat, I'd looked up into the trees.

One of my friends screeched. "He's looking for Drop Bears!"

Squeals of laughter came from my Australian friends who were rolling on their backs. A tough way to find out that Drop Bears were a yarn based on Koala Bears that would get stoned on eucalyptus, lose their grip and fall out of trees. Harmless gentle creatures.

Infuriated that I'd been caught out by the national joke, I made it my mission to trick all Aussies into believing we had giant woodlice in Britain, that killed more people than sharks did in Australia. I enrolled other English travellers to help me spin the yarn – and we became good at it.

I discovered that the art of instilling myth seemed to be no more than repetition from different sources – giving utter fabrication, fabric.

I was relieved to realise the manager's story as just part of a larger Brazilian myth, told in the same way we tell our children fear-inducing fairy tales to stop them entering the woods at night – or walking off with strangers. I guessed this Brazilian story had been designed to keep the street kids in check and make sure they knew their place and behaved.

I smiled to myself, happy again, realising a few good myths make this crazy world go round.

Soon our vegetable buying was complete and now burdened with our heavy shopping, we started our walk back.

Barely fifty metres from the shop, the manager started elbowing me and whispered.

"Did you see me?"

"Huh?"

"Did you see what I did? You didn't, did you?"

Perplexed, I asked again. "See what?"

He looked back at the shop furtively, then reached into his pocket and showed me something in the palm of his hand.

A single bulb of garlic.

Looking all around to make sure no-one was watching, he popped the garlic back in his pocket. "Crazy prices. No way was I going to pay for that."

He appeared happy with my blank look.

"I knew you'd not seen me. Nor them. I'm good, aren't I?"

It dawned on me. Our hotel manager, wanna-be bandit-assassin, the street-kid-killing cop on sabbatical, was in fact, just a petty thief. A man whom some Austrian lady had asked to house-sit her decaying pension.

With a straight face, I just smiled at him kindly. "Yup. Never saw a thing. That was magic," I said.

He smiled all the way back home. I'd made his day. As we passed back by the seaside road, the kids again moved away like a flock of pigeons, resettling once we were out of sight.

From outside the pension, we could hear laughter coming from within. As we stepped back inside, we found Luciana and the Austrian co-owner had cracked a bottle of wine. They invited us to join them with a glass and accepting, we tucked into the food preparation.

The crabs were still alive and needed to be cleaned before being popped into the boiling water, which was also delegated as a man's job. I moved as quickly as possible to reduce any suffering. Worried that I didn't have the right technique, I looked over to see how the manager was doing his.

I froze.

I watched as he placed a crab on its back and sunk the blade into its belly. He used his whole body weight to lean on the knife and then turned it left and right slowly. As the knife moved back and forth, the eyes of the crabs were reaching out on their stems, retracting with each turn. The manager's tongue, hanging out just slightly, shook mirroring each movement of the crab's contortions.

He sensed me transfixed, watching him.

"Look," he said without his eyes moving off the crab. "When I turn the knife. Watch."

He was almost in a trance, breathing in short sharp breaths.

The hairs stood up on my arms and my stomach turned.

In that moment I knew, without a doubt, that everything he had told us, down to the smallest detail – was completely and utterly true. He was a killer who not only enjoyed killing – with each life that faded away, he gained energy.

That night, as we slept, Luciana awoke on hearing someone in our room. She caught the silhouette of a young boy, maybe eleven or twelve who on seeing her awake, vanished as quickly as he'd appeared.

Due to the jewellery with us, we'd also chosen the pension as it had seemed theft-tight. Clueless to how they'd entered, we could only guess they'd been let in.

With two reasons to leave, our bags were packed within an hour, and we moved into a new pension at the other end of town.

Able to speak the basics of Portuguese, Luciana now with the bit between her teeth, set out to unravel the mystery. Charming anyone and everyone, from the stallholders to the street-kids, it barely took her a few hours to piece the jigsaw together and confirm our fears.

Yes, the man was a policeman from Rio who was on paid sabbatical for bringing in a bounty. Yes, he was the manager, and he was in partnership with the Austrian lady – but their enterprise was not rooms. Using his reputation and contacts, he'd taken over the local drug trade. The hotel was just a base and cover for his dealings. The craziest bit? The street-kids, his very victims, were also his street-dealers. They'd come to the pension late at night to collect their commission and pick up more wares to sell. This had been going on ever since we'd arrived and we'd not seen or heard a thing.

The previous night, due to the celebratory drink-fuelled barbecue, one of the kids, sensing his bosses were not as sharp as normal, had taken his chance to sneak into our room and try his luck. We'd, of course, told the manager what had happened, before realising the full implications, and were now worried for the child – whoever he was.

The policeman from Rio wasn't just an assassin. He wasn't just a child killer. He was someone who took pleasure in ending life and sending spirits back to where they had come from. His inadequacies were so deep, he elicited fear and mistook a petrified smile for giving him the godlike right to choose life or death. He killed kids for stealing food and dealing drugs, yet he stole food and sold drugs. A damaged man who, like any little boy, just wanted to hear the words, 'Well done.' The happiest I saw him was when I'd complimented him on his ability to steal a bulb of garlic.

This man had found his niche in life. He was happy. His bosses were happy. He was a Rio cop who moonlighted as a murderer for hire.

We soon headed to another town further down the coast where I scrubbed my skin hard to get clean of a deep dirty grease-like sensation that was taking time to fade. Recalling his face, words or stories, within an instant brought back the sensation of queasiness.

As we moved out of Brazil and into the Andes, I brought up the story countless times and asked locals what they knew about the subject. Apparently, Colombia was the same as Brazil – if not worse. We heard how shopkeepers, who had a problem with street-kids and petty theft, would hire a policeman to solve the issue. The police would turn up in the middle of the night and throw a grenade amongst the sleeping children. Injured survivors would be shot. Problem over. The police report would state the deaths had been caused by a rival gang infighting, or something similar. No investigation. Situation solved.

The police never left witnesses.
They could not afford to.

The bitter taste of his words were still at the back of my throat.

My stomach still queasy.

So, choosing a taxi in Bogotá airport with a policeman asleep inside was a mistake.

A big mistake.

I knew better.

But it was too late.

BOGOTÁ – ILLOGICAL INTUITION

WHEN WE TOLD our taxi driver the address of our hotel, he just yawned, nodded and started the engine. As we pulled away I looked back again, to see the policeman. He'd vanished. The two taxi drivers leaning against the light pole, with cigarettes still in their mouths had not moved. They stared after us. Above them, small clouds of their cigarette smoke hung in the still night air, refusing to disperse.

The mythical dangers of Bogotá airport were alive in my mind. My eyes searched for signs that correlated with the warnings. There it was. A barrier blocking the road. A policeman holding a clipboard. The checkpoint. Our insurance policy. I breathed in and as I breathed out, a wave of peace flowed throughout my body.

The taxi driver gently slowed to a halt wound his window down. Bending to peer in, the policeman's questioning tone was clear. Although unable to make out a word, I could tell he was satisfied with our driver's mumbled reply. Our passports were at the ready alongside my expectant smile, but his eyes did not so much as flicker towards me. Or more worryingly, to the long legs of the beautiful girl in the back. The policeman muttered a few words to the driver and waved for us to continue on our way. The driver calmly accelerated out of the airport.

Putting on a strong south-west of England accent, that Luciana had heard me use many times as a vocal disguise, I hissed. "What'd he say?"

"Huh?"

"Luciana, what did he say to the driver? That was the checkpoint."

"What was?"

"Luciana!"

The taxi driver raised a lazy eyebrow, his body language clear – 'Not another late night domestic in my taxi'.

Pivoting in my seat, I turned to face the rear. I widened my eyes and mouthed the words. "What did they say?"

"I wasn't listening," she whispered, delving into her hand-bag. "I can't find my lip gloss. Have you seen it?"

An internal survival alarm flashed red. My cheeks tingled as they filled with blood. Sitting back down into my seat, the taxi driver seemed as calm as could be. Luciana was still busy, head deep in her bag foraging. Everything appeared perfectly normal. I tried to relax.

Outside the airport, we pulled onto the main dual carriageway and a second alarm was immediately triggered.

When choosing our hotel in downtown Bogotá, I'd committed a visual memory of the route to mind. We'd just turned left out of the airport. We should have turned right. I was sure of it.

I called loudly and clearly. "Luciana."

I broke up each word speaking loudly and clearly so the taxi driver would grasp that I was aware that he'd gone the wrong way.

"Can – you – check – our – map – please?"

I knew we had no map. I also knew Luciana knew we had no map. I figured that by asking for the map that we both knew we didn't have, that she would figure that something was up.

Luciana looked up from her handbag.

"We – don't – have – a – map?"

Here I was, in South America with a South American girlfriend, who not only spoke fluent Spanish but was streetwise and fiercely capable of holding her own. The same girl that could sense a thief near us at ten feet. And the same girl whose image in my eye had terrified the south London muggers into returning my money. Yet, in this time of great need, she was completely and totally oblivious. I bottled up a scream that would have been so loud it would have woken her Incan ancestors.

This had to be dealt with alone. I needed to up the stakes and confront the taxi driver. Let him know that I knew he was going the wrong way. It was time to man-up and stop the hints.

"Excuse me, sir. But I think we have gone the wrong way."

I pointed over my shoulder in the opposite direction. "I believe our hotel is that way."

Wincing, I waited for his response – the long exhalation of air caused by this tediously boring tourist who arrives on this first day in a city and has the obnoxious audacity to tell an experienced taxi driver that he is driving the wrong way.

I was cringing.

To my surprise, he pulled a sharp U-turn. So sudden it made me grip the door handle and hold my breath. The other cars touched their brakes or adjusted their steering to avoid us, seemingly used to such manoeuvres. Not even one honked a horn. Our driver came across as relaxed as ever. Luciana was still burrowing in her handbag looking for the missing lip gloss.

Only I, the lone sane Englishman, in this continent of craziness, was uptight.

Consoling myself, I was at least glad we were now heading the right way into the city. Well, as far as I could tell. Then, a sign saying 'Bogotá Centro' confirmed it. I should have been happy but my mind was racing as neurones were fired away desperate to make connections. In addition to the previous two warning lights that were still flashing inside my head, an internal siren was now beeping. The alarm was connected to a memory that wanted my attention. The U-turn had not been smooth. He had turned in a series of sharp swerves, correcting each one, before the next. So instead of making a circular movement with an effortless curve, we'd turned in a series of straight lines, as if circumnavigating a polygon.

I'd experienced this before.

Images flashed through my mind.

The smell of aniseed.

A sharp taste at the back of my throat.

Laughter.

There she was.

Clearly labelled.

A memory under 'Turkey, Cappadocia, 1988'.

TURKISH DELIGHT

AFTER MY FIRST year as a student at film school, with a long summer break and a little saved, I set out to hitchhike to the far corner of Europe where I wished to set foot in Asia.

After hitchhiking some two thousand five hundred miles from London to Istanbul via Copenhagen and Berlin, I ended up in the heart of central Anatolia – in a town called Göreme. The area was famous for tall, pointed, limestone white rocks that rose out of the ground like stalagmites many metres high. Halfway up these giant reversed icicles, were doors and windows since many had been hollowed out to make houses. Rope ladders had been used for access, making them perfectly secure. They had been occupied until the 50s when a devastating earthquake had caused many to collapse and the area had been abandoned.

On this day, in particular, I'd spent the day exploring the underground city of Derinkuyu. An ancient complex, also hand-carved out of bare rock, sixteen floors deep that had been able to hide up to twenty thousand people from prying eyes.

Fascinated by the maze of corridors, rooms and air vents, I'd hung around later than the last bus and now needed to hitch a ride back to base. Eventually, a beat-up, old white Mercedes Sedan stopped for me. The car was pointing the wrong way. The occupants, two young men with easy smiles, assured me that I should come for the ride as they would soon be returning in Göreme. The Turks were the friendliest and most hospitable people I'd ever come across. They would do anything to help a stranger. I jumped in, making it the only time I'd hitched a lift heading the wrong way.

The two guys laughed and teased each other. As we barrelled down the perfectly straight road, gently weaving from one side of the road to the other, it slowly dawned on me that they might have been drinking. The man in the passenger seat turned around. "My friend. He drives not bad. His first time driving. He good, huh?"

I used my friendliest smile to hide the fact I was taken aback. "Yes, not bad."

Which was worse? Getting a lift with someone drunk? Or getting a lift with someone who was behind the wheel for the very first time?

The man in the passenger seat opened the glovebox and took a swig from a bottle. He passed it to the driver who took a glug and handed the bottle to me. "Raki?"

I accepted the offer and took a big swig straight from the bottle. The fresh anise flavour, backed by the kick of the forty per cent proof spirits, immediately made things feel a lot better. Besides, the road was straight and the surrounding land was flat and barren. There were no cliffs to drive off, or trees to drive into. The road was empty of cars. It was just us.

The driver gently swerved crossing over the white line, as he got used to the steering. Starting to explore the dashboard, he randomly tried levers and knobs. He indicated left, then right – popped on the hazards and flashed the headlights. There was a moment of panic as the washers smeared his dusty windscreen and blocked his vision until his friend flicked on the wipers and cleared the blurred screen. Pressing the horn made him jump. Pure slapstick comedy. Each action seemed funnier than the previous until his friend checked his watch and announced, "Time to go back."

He slowed the car and pulled a wide U-turn, bouncing off the road into the dry fields. He made the manoeuvre by yanking the steering wheel then straightening it, before yanking it again, and again straightening it. The car bounced back onto the sealed road leaving a cloud of dust behind us. We were finally pointing back towards Göreme. The driver pushed the accelerator to the floor, and the engine growled. Both men screamed with delight and the raki bottle was soon empty.

Arriving on the outskirts of Göreme they pulled up and swapped seats.

I jumped out as I could easily walk the rest of the way home. Barely thirty minutes after having met, we bid each other a warm farewell, the tears of laughter still in our eyes – our momentary friendship bonded by laughter and the raki.

14

BOGOTÁ – SYMPATHY FOR THE DEVIL

THE ACTIONS of the U-turn in Turkey were identical to the U-turn our taxi driver had just made. I had matched the driving characteristics of a man who could not drive, with the professional taxi driver sat next to me.

Something was wrong.

Another thing was bothering me.

The engine.

It was revving too high for our speed. Although driving at 60mph, we were still in third gear.

I took stock of the situation again. Luciana busied herself filing her fingernails. The taxi driver, with one elbow out of the window, steered with one hand, as casually as if he'd been driving all his life. No-one had a care in the world, except me.

I reminded myself that this was Bogotá, not London. That Colombian taxi drivers might not have taken something like London's infamously difficult black taxicab test. The cabs here were probably not even required to have a licence. If they were, a driver could maybe pay a bribe for one. Or use a counterfeit licence. Anything needed to work.

That was it. It explained everything.

Overwhelmed with sympathy, I realised the man I'd doubted was just trying to earn a decent day's living. No-one chooses the graveyard shift for pleasure. Maybe he had kids fast asleep at home and was working after-hours so he could afford to fill their bellies and send them to school.

It was late. I was tired and had obviously become a touch paranoid. I remembered the T-shirt my mother had bought me – 'Just Because I'm Paranoid, It Doesn't Mean They Ain't After Me'.

My own mother mocking me.

But, perhaps, I was paranoid. But maybe they were still after me?

I ramped up the logic and reminded myself that we were in the Americas. In Europe, we thought automatic cars were for old ladies or people that struggled to drive. This was a manual gear-shift car. It was possible that our driver had learnt to drive in an automatic. If so he had never needed to listen to the engine revs and change gear accordingly.

Feeling kindness instead of fear, I reached to the gear stick and mimed pulling it back in the fourth gear.

The driver raised an eyebrow by the width of an eyelash and slipped the gear stick back into the fourth – as if he was doing it just to keep me happy.

Can't win. Classic Latino macho pride.

Yet, as the high-pitch revolutions of the engine settled back down – so did I.

Overriding the alerts in my head, my logic took control of

the situation and manually turned off these false alarms, one by one.

Leaning back into my seat I set my eyes forward and started to soak up the views of the night-time road. The city centre was becoming closer with every minute as we cruised under brightly lit overhead signs naming each passing suburb. Small shops started to appear. Even though closed, they produced the warm fuzzy sense of familiarity. Signalling the universal, bustling, commercial needs of mankind. Advertisements promised offerings of fresh vegetables, good clothes and tasty snacks once daylight returned. Through these shop signs, with their characteristic lettering, words and colour – Bogotá was giving me the first glimpse of her character. She started to feel like any other city I'd been to.

I reminded myself again that it was easy to get the wrong end of a stick in a foreign country. Bogotá's reputation had just got under my skin. People are always nervous of the unknown. One man's strange city is another man's home. Some perspective was needed.

I filled my lungs with air and breathed out slowly emptying my lungs.

It had been a long day.

I let myself think about home.

15

A MATTER OF PERSPECTIVE

A FAR-DISTANT AND strange country is struck by a plague or terror. From animal-born flu to dirty water-induced cholera, or from crop-eating locusts to man-killing wasps, or some other 'end-of-the-world' apocalyptic scenario. Occurrences that give people something to talk about over a coffee break and curb any ambition to travel. Stories that keep people content, right where they are, safe in their home country.

In May 1994, the newspapers and TV news-shows of South America, as well as around the world, were filled with the screaming headlines of a new horror.

'Highly Infectious Disease Outbreak!'

'Flesh-eating Bacteria!'

'Zombie Plague – Many Dead!'

An outbreak of a killer bug was apparently causing people to drop like flies. Death awaited the victims of the 'Zombie virus' within forty-eight hours.

Could this be a monkey virus from the deepest darkest

jungles of Africa? A mysterious parasite from the depths of the Amazon? A radical disease released from a freshly opened ancient tomb from the jungles of Burma?

No. This outbreak came from England. The epicentre of 'The Zombie Plague' being the quaint Cotswold town of Stroud, nestled in her five valleys made famous by Laurie Lee's novel, *Cider with Rosie*. Stroud also happened to be where we would be returning to see my mother within three days.

On hearing we were still going to return home as planned, our South American friends thought we were crazy.

Marianna, who whilst under lockdown due to a running gun battle, had joked about being pushed out of a taxi, pleaded with Luciana. "Stay here. Don't go back to England. It's dangerous. You will die."

Stroud wasn't a faraway abstract concept. I knew the shop-keepers, teachers, landlords and doctors. The people of Stroud were my people.

They tracked the outbreak to the local hospital, where my mother worked. She'd sent an airmail letter explaining that our cherished family doctor – who'd not only looked after us through our childhood but had cared for her parents – had caught the infection from a patient. To save his life, they amputated his leg up to the hip.

The disease, necrotising fasciitis, was real enough, yet we had not flinched from the idea of returning.

Home is home. Life was going on in Stroud as normal. And life in Bogotá, a city of eight or so million, was also going on as normal.

Barely an hour had passed since we landed. I was fresh in the city, an outsider, whose heart had been beating fast, driven by fear of the unknown.

Yup, it's all a matter of perspective.

BOGOTÁ – THE HOME STRAIGHT

WE WERE NOW on the main boulevard heading into the heart of Bogotá. Our hotel was further down this road. Like many cities of the Americas, Bogotá was built on a grid system. A criss-cross network of avenues and cross streets labelled with numbers instead of names. Being a first-timer without a map, this made it easy to get orientated. Our hotel, according to my handwritten note, was on the intersection of the nineteenth avenue and fifth street. Already on the nineteenth avenue, we were passing the thirty-third cross street. We just needed to stay on the same road and count down. Twenty-eight more blocks to go. I guessed within a quarter of an hour or so, we'd be in bed, thankful that I'd not scared Luciana with my paranoia.

Now passing shops with large window displays that spilt light onto the night street, I marvelled at the patience of the shop mannequins as they stared onto these empty pavements awaiting tomorrow's shoppers.

The twenty-seventh cross street passed us by, then the twenty-sixth.

Recognising some shop's brand names, I imagined how a tourist from Bogotá would feel driving at night into London for the first time. Greeted by the same brand names and similarly brightly lit shop windows. Filled with similar mannequins, frozen in London time. How would one of London's black cab drivers treat someone with broken English fresh out of Colombia? Images of London, pubs and that pint of stout I'd missed for the last half-year, filled my mind. Still wired, a cold beer sounded better than bed. Once we'd checked in, maybe Luciana would be willing for us to find a bar and grab a late-night drink? Then again she was almost asleep in the back of the taxi. Maybe I'd have to have a beer alone.

The twenty-fourth cross over street passed us by, followed by the twenty-third.

Ten more minutes and we'd be checking in. Chuckling at all the crazy doubts and fears that a man can suffer alone, I reasoned two beers were needed to rinse away the madness. Then I'd sleep well. Yep, we deserved it.

With a flick of his wrist, the taxi driver suddenly turned a sharp right into a derelict and dark backstreet. There were no street lights. There were no other cars. Large empty cardboard boxes lay broken and scattered – bottles and rubbish slowed our way. The driver reduced our speed to a crawl. Was he trying to avoid the trash? Could he not see ahead? He looked to his right. My eyes followed his. Silhouettes of men loomed up from the darkness. They were walking towards us. He peered to his left. Shadowy figures were stooping to look into our vehicle. They looked like zombies. Our driver was not afraid of them. Quite the opposite. He was lowering his head so he could look up through the windscreen and see their faces with ease.

He was looking for somebody.

These shadow-like creatures were reaching out for the door handles of our car.

All doubt evaporated.

Our driver was a delivery-man.

And we were the goods being delivered.

To the abattoir.

The black-hole of Bogotá.

We were moments from joining 'The Disappeared'.

Then I saw it.

The knife.

A long, shiny knife blade – being held to the throat of our taxi driver.

A tsunami of adrenalin surged through me.

Even if a robbery had been expected. Even if all the other travellers had warned me – this had no match to all the information I'd gleaned from many a late-night travelling tale. This situation was different to all the scenarios that had played out in my head.

This moment in time was unique.

This was an emergency.

A real emergency.

And I didn't have the faintest notion of what to do next.

Not a clue.

Because the hand gripping the handle of the knife was mine.

I was holding my Swiss army lock-blade knife to our taxi driver's neck.

I calculated the speed of the zombie-men's hands reaching towards the door handles.

We had three seconds.

Then it was game over.

Time slowed down to a snail's pace so that my mind had no need to race. The image of the knife in front of me lingered lazily, moving frame by frame. I now had plenty of time to sift through a lifetime of memories, searching to find a solution.

I'd hit the Pause Button.

17

THE PATTERN SEEKER

A SECOND HAD BEEN USED *up.*

Two seconds left.

The events had been relived.

Each memory held meaning.

But nothing made sense.

I could find no answer.

Maybe this was the end?

If it was, it wasn't over just yet.

First, I needed to release the pause button and re-enter normal time.

Take a deep breath and live out the last moments.

Save my last words for Luciana.

'I'm sorry.'

'Don't worry.'

'I love you.'

Maybe I could hold her hand?

Assure her she would not feel pain.

That it will all be over quickly.

. . .

I'd given up

Time, even the three seconds, lost all significance.

Each memory played on an endless loop as if on its own gravity-free screen.

Then I heard that voice again.

Relax. Watch. Observe.

The events freed from my rearranging, moved of their own accord. New strands grew between each image, forming a three-dimensional cobweb of light. The strands contracted, pulling these experiences together, creating links in ways I had not foreseen.

The dots were being connected.

The face of Luciana's brother merged with that of the taxi driver.

The driver now had the eyes of Angel.

A reminder.

The cruel twist of fate.

The scars.

Some worse than others.

Unhealed, raw and ugly.

Behind each wound.

Love hiding.

Trying to reconnect.

There it was.

    The answer.

    The truth.

    Respect.

    Love.

    Man to man.

    Human to human.

    Five simple words.

    Words to be spoken, slowly and clearly.

    Two seconds left.

    Enough time.

    Just.

    I hit the pause button – releasing us from ultra-slow motion – restarting the sensation of normal time.

    Deep breath.

    Ready?

    Yep.

    Go!

18

FIVE WORDS

A TWITCH UNDER MY EYE.

The stench of the derelict rubbish-strewn streets hit me.

I was back. The alleyway. The zombie-men. Bogotá's abattoir.

The taxi driver with my knife to his neck.

The five Spanish words in my mind.

On the tip of my tongue.

Filling my lungs, I let the words roll.

"*No quiero no problemas, Señor.*"

I'd done it.

Not a word of German.

Spoken as calmly as if asking directions on a Sunday walk in the park.

But damn.

The sentence was a double negative.

'I don't want no problems, Mister', literally meaning 'I do want problems, Mister'.

The driver was in no place to pull me up on bad grammar. The knife was my translator, and he understood perfectly.

He tilted his head a fraction, lifting his jaw slightly away from the knife. Each muscle on his face static. His eyes didn't flicker a millimetre. He just stared forwards.

This guy was as cool as ice.

The fingers of the zombie-men's hands widened ready to grip our door handles and squeeze them open.

What was the driver thinking?

How long would it take him to reach for his gun?

Could he pull his knife in time?

Speaking the words had used up a second.

One second left!

Then I saw it.

A small muscle quivered momentarily, as it tugged at his eyelid.

His eye had twitched.

The *hijo-de-puta* had hit his pause button.

19

THE LAST SECOND

STUCK in a micro-second of real-time panic with my gaze locked on our taxi driver, he casually sifted through a life's worth of experiences.

Wrestling in the street as a child.

Tackling the big kid.

Winning his first fight.

His mother calling his name.

His father beating him with a stick.

Trying to learn things at school.

Wondering why nothing made sense.

The first inhalation from a stolen cigarette.

The moment his parents first let him down.

The first strange feeling when a girl smiled at him.

Getting laughed at by other kids.

Understanding the power of money.

Realising that things could be stolen.

The wild sensation of a first kiss.

The pain of being beaten to a pulp.

The injustice where the wrong gets rewarded.

The indignation when the right gets punished.

Learning to break the rules.

Realising he was a man, not a boy.

Looking in a mirror and seeing an outlaw.

Living in a new world.

A new boss.

Under new rules.

Caught in an alternative system.

A system with less mercy than the last.

Trapped.

A deliveryman.

Wearing the clothes of a taxi driver.

With the heart of the grim reaper.

Half a second left.

My mind raced.

He hadn't seen my knife.

He could only sense it.

He didn't know who I was.

What had happened in my life.

We were both strangers.

We could only guess about the other.

Was he thinking of me as a rich-foreigner-kid bluffing?

Was he stronger than me? A better fighter? Could he over-power me?

Was he calculating the micro-seconds before the disposal team opened our doors?

Would I make a mistake? Would I turn to confront them, giving him a chance to attack me?

What did he have to lose?

Did he even care about his own life?

I needed him to think about his children.

If he didn't have any kids, I needed him to dream about the ones he might have.

I needed him to want to sing the song he'd never yet written.

To want to live, to see his dreams come true.

He knew as well as I did that once the zombie-men had the doors open, there was no escape.

He also knew that with one movement of my wrist, I could take him with me.

We could all live.

We could all die.

The first of the zombie-men's hands reached for Luciana's door handle.

A click as the lock was released.

The muscle under the driver's eye tugged at his eyelid.

His eye had twitched.

A decision made.

His jaw muscle swelled as he gritted his teeth.

The engine roared.

The zombie-men yelped and jumped back and out of the way as he powered the vehicle towards the light at the end of the block.

As some crazy, yet instinctive way of saying 'thank you,' I lowered the knife from his neck to his kidneys.

Not a sound, word or murmur from inside the car. Not one of us breathing.

Me? Pulled a knife?

An impossibility. Yet whatever I preferred to think, a knife was currently being held by my hand. My hand was attached to my arm. My arm was attached to my shoulder, and presumably still controlled by my mind.

There was no escaping from this.

The impossible was possible.

It had happened.

He was driving us away.

I moved my left hand to cover the blade, hoping that it would appear less threatening.

Then, realising this might make me appear weak, I uncovered it.

The blade freaked me out, so I covered it again, settling for the comfort of not being able to see the reality of what I was actually doing. I told myself to sit calmly, not fidget, and appear as if this was something I did every week.

At the end of the block, he turned right into a street with some lighting, but still too run-down for comfort. The next right took us down another derelict road. One last right-hand turn completed all sides of the square, bringing us back onto the main Avenue Nineteen. Again, we were heading back into town, towards our hotel.

Everything was the same as it had been barely a minute before. The same empty pavements. The same shop mannequins with the expressions of poker players, watching us. The same hum from the engine as we cut through the silence of Bogotá at sleep.

Everything the same, except for the knife being held to the kidneys of our taxi driver – the blade covered out of sight as if by a professional kidnapper.

Until this moment, Luciana had been completely silent. With the force of a machine gun, a torrent of high-speed Spanish erupted. Each word laced with venom, designed to wound and cut deep. Each syllable piercing his skull, threatening his sanity. Each sentence wrapping itself around his neck and tightening. The words disabling his ability to think— leaving him only capable of driving.

Luciana and I were finally working as the perfect team. I had rendered him incapable of moving, and Luciana had rendered him incapable of thinking.

Re-orientating myself, again I counted down the cross streets. We passed the fifteenth, then the fourteenth. The buildings on either side of the road growing taller. The streets gaining life. The ninth, then the eighth. Even at this time in the morning, these downtown streets had several people walking on either side of the roads. Back in the land of normality, we slowed to a halt on the crossover with the fifth street.

We'd arrived.

To our left, the bright sign of our hotel shone. Although never seen before, the name alone filled my heart with the warmth of a homecoming.

The taxi driver opened the boot and unloaded our rucksacks onto the pavement as if nothing had happened. Luciana was still at full volume with her tirade. She was verbally undressing him in public. The truth of his actions naked, and in the open for all to witness. The commotion brought the owner of the hotel out onto the top of the hotel steps.

I quietly folded the knife, fumbling to get it back into the knife holder that had barely been on my belt twenty-four hours.

Should I pay him? We'd agreed on a price. I didn't want any hard feelings. He had dropped us at the hotel. Besides, I could prove nothing. Because nothing had happened. He'd just taken the wrong turn and some helpful men had come towards the car to help us on our way. It wasn't their fault they looked like extras out of a zombie movie. I paid the driver and motioned that he should keep the change. He'd not spoken a single word from when we'd first entered the taxi. And he didn't speak a word now. Although he didn't meet my eye, I caught the smallest recognition. A tiny movement of his head that could have been mistaken for a nod.

I slung a rucksack over each shoulder – wrestled with the day bags – and started to cross the road.

The driver climbed back into his taxi and drove away.

Luciana, already with the hotel owner, was recounting the recent events, gesticulating wildly.

The hotel owner started to laugh.

Loudly.

I knew it. I had pulled a knife on some poor taxi driver who had got lost. He was probably driving straight to the police. He had friends in the police. And he knew where we were staying.

I felt a fool. Exhausted, I dropped the bags in front of the two of them. The manager fired questions at Luciana, whose eyes still wide with indignation was answering him with enough volume to wake half the neighbourhood.

The manager turned to me.

"He drove you off the main road? Which cross street?"

"Twentieth. Maybe nineteenth."

The hotel owner threw his head back and roared with laughter. He shook his hand back and forth with a loose wrist as if he'd burnt his fingers.

"Block twenty!" He pointed at me incredulously. "You pulled a knife on block twenty?" He whistled to catch the night porter's attention. "Come listen to this!"

Now, not only trying to dislocate his wrist, he blew air out from his mouth as if he'd eaten a super hot chilli.

The night porter arrived.

The owner pointed at us as if zoo exhibits, motioning to Luciana that she should speak.

"Tell the porter what he did!"

Barely able to contain his amusement, he beckoned to me.

"And you Inglés loco, show us your knife."

I opened the popper and presented the Swiss army knife in my palm.

The laughter had now infected the night porter.

Slightly demeaned, I opened the blade and showed them how it locked – the perfect boy-scout knife for slicing through a loaf of bread in one go. This seemed to amuse them even more.

The owner fought to control himself.

"And tell me again, what did you say to the driver?"

I repeated my five words.

"No quiero no problemas, Señor."

The two men's legs seemed to lose strength. They grabbed at each other to keep themselves upright.

Although their hysterics were infectious, I could not bring myself to return even the smallest of smiles. I'd just had the worst hour of my life. And they thought it funny. I was broken. All my energy spent.

Yet again, I'd managed to do it all backwards. Instead of returning home with stories of having suffered theft and banditry, I was to return with a story of accidentally scaring the life out of some poor innocent driver and car-jacking his taxi. As far as sharing travel stories over cups of tea with my mother, I marked this one as censored. Highly confidential. To be erased from all mother-son records.

Maybe it wasn't that bad? At least I'd paid the driver. I'd even given him a tip.

The owner, wiping the tears from his eyes, nodded for the porter to take our bags to our room. As if old friends, he put an arm each around each of us, and guided us inside.

"For you two, drinks are on the house."

As the owner organised our beverages, he kept mumbling the words, shaking his head in disbelief. As if the phrase had been the best punch-line to a joke that he'd ever come across. "No quiero no problemas, Señor."

Luciana was grinning, her black eyes glistening. She gave me one of her smiles. The ear to ear grin that could tame a thousand men.

"He's right. Best Spanish you ever spoke."

I shuffled, leaning backwards on my seat.

"But why were you were so quiet?"

" I thought you'd you'd lost it. When I saw your knife. Of course, I didn't know what to say!"

I ignored the fresh chuckles from the hotel owner.

"So why did you scream at him?"

"Because I realised. When we came back on the main road."

We both stared at her.

Luciana shrugged defensively.

"We are not like you. If you accuse a Latino of something. And they haven't done it. They go mad!"

The hotel owner nodded.

Luciana continued.

"When the driver didn't say anything. When he kept driving. Then I knew. You had got it right."

She swivelled the palms of her hands upwards.

"Of course I screamed his head off!"

The owner moved his gaze from me to Luciana, and back again.

"Inglés. Are you sure it was Calle 19?"

"I was counting the streets down to arrive here. More or less. Yes."

His face quivered, caught somewhere between a frown and merriment.

We watched him in silence as he methodically added some ice to the rum, topped the drink with cola and pushed the glass towards Luciana. Turning to a glass-fronted fridge, he pulled out two cans of beer, crispy white with frost. Keeping one for himself, he slid the other to me.

Opened in perfect synchronicity, the cans hissed, then clunked, as we slammed them together.

"Salud!"

"Cheers!"

The ice-cold bubbles burned my mouth. I was overcome with a sense of relief. I'd never tasted a beer so good.

He finished his in one long glug, crushed the can and slammed it down on the table.

His eyes were on fire with delight.

"And you. Inglés loco. I want to hear it one more time."

With a wink, he nodded towards the fridge full of beers.

"And, I want to hear the whole story. All the way from the beginning."

Q - How long is a second?

A - It depends.

THE END

Thank you for taking the time to read
3 Seconds in Bogotá

If you enjoy feel-good stories with slightly open endings that tease the imagination, then close this book... and again, thank you.
If you can spare a moment, please leave an honest review on your favourite online bookstore and/or **Goodreads.**

However, if you wish to know more of the grittier details of the back streets of Bogotá in the '90s – or wish to check some links concerning the conspiracies, locations and more famous incidents mentioned within the story – then turn to the next pages...

STORIES BEHIND THE STORIES - EPILOGUE

Stories Behind the Stories
is for those that have read
3 Seconds in Bogotá
and wish to know a little more.

QUARTER CENTURY LATER

From the safety of a quarter of a decade later, it is interesting to compare memories. Some as vivid as if they had happened yesterday, others fading like the pattern on fabric left out in the sun.

Other than vague images of cathedrals and colourful markets down side lanes, our last two days in Bogotá remain forgotten. The memory of the flight home has also evaporated into the ether.

A few months later, I do remember walking across the footbridge from London's Charing Cross towards the South-bank, when I'd become aware of a heaviness in my pocket. The Swiss army tool kit from my cub-scout days had gained new memories and meaning. Before I could change my mind, the penknife was cart-wheeling through the sky towards a watery burial. The barely visible splash filled me with disappointment. The knife was gone, yet the incident remained etched into my mind with questions still lurking in the shadows.

As the years rolled by, I only shared the tale with trusted friends under special circumstances. They had to know me well enough to understand the event as a one-off, and not something I often did on late nights in London to save on taxi fare home.

* * *

Twenty-five years later, I hit the button.

This time not the pause button, but the publish button.

The story now entrusted with strangers for the first time.

A wild feeling.

Amongst favourable feedback, a familiar question started to appear.

"I love your book, but what really happened?"

Each time, I'd reply the same.

"This is a true story. I only know what I know. How can I tell you more than what I have already told you?""

Some nodded.

Others shook their heads in dismay.

* * *

My childhood best friend called me.

"I really liked the story. Especially the beginning and the middle," he said.

I knew perfectly well what that meant.

"What's wrong?"

There was a slight pause.

He added, "Well, I was kind of expecting more."

"More what!?"

"More," he affirmed.

"Like?"

"I was kind of hoping it would end up in a big knife fight."

"A knife fight!?"

"Yes!" He sounded excited. "Like in a real thriller."

I took a deep breath.

"A real thriller? This is a true story. My story! If there had been a knife fight. I wouldn't be here today talking to you, would I?"

"Well, you could make something up?"

Frustrated that I'd missed something so obvious, he added a deep sigh to drive his point home.

I sighed back, feeling he'd missed the whole point of the story.

"No, I'm not making up a James Bond, goodie-versus-baddie knife fight!'"

This went on for weeks.

* * *

Three things slowly dawned on me.

Firstly, a group of people wanted to know more of what was going on in those back streets. They required the story to be wrapped up.

Secondly, I realised that as time had passed, I'd popped the understanding of the events along with any remaining questions into the deep freezer of time, and had never wanted to find out more.

The potential darkness of the story repelled me.

I was attracted to the magical elements.

Life had somehow given the tools needed for us to survive the encounter. How had the crucial leather knife holder been given to me barely a day or so before? A 'coincidence' beyond coincidences.

Thirdly, as I'd now published the story to a wide audience, it was time to uncover more and deliver what they requested.

Slightly resentful, I figured, if they want blood, I'll give them blood.

I had little idea the research would reveal enough to push the story through the boundaries of classic thriller or James Bond goody-versus-baddie heroism and into the realms of utter horror.

THE MILLIONAIRE'S RIDE

I now knew a little more than had been told in the book.

I had one eye peeled for relevant stories in the media. The taxi scam had been updated into modern times, now so infamous, it had even earned a name. The taxi scam was now known as the Passeo Millonario, or the Millionaire's Ride.

Travellers no longer carried cash; they stored finances within banks, accessed by plastic cards and protected by PIN codes. The modern urban highwaymen's secret to instant riches now lay in obtaining the card's four magic numbers.

The taxi drivers' 'assistants' now guided their charges under a knife to the nearest ATM, where their bank accounts were emptied one by one.

The scam came to worldwide attention in 2013, when CIA agent and DEA operative John Watson took the Millionaire's Ride in Bogotá. John put up a fight, but in the ensuing struggle was stabbed four times and left for dead on the pavement of a rich suburb. He was pronounced DOA at the hospital.

This time, the full might of the US security agencies set out to reap justice for one of their own and, using a large cash bounty as a catalyst, his murderers were soon in court.

Was the Colombia of the early '90s really so bad?

Football fans might remember the other Escobar of 1994.

The 27-year-old footballer Andrés Escobar had been playing for the national Colombian team in the World Cup when he scored an own goal. Many blamed his mistake for the Colombian team's elimination from the tournament.

On 2 July 1994, they shot Escobar six times with a .38 pistol with the assassin shouting "Goal!" after each shot.

The wild madness of this incident alone paints a picture.

My modern-day research started with a call to a friend who had married a Colombian and was now living in Bogotá.

On hearing the description of the alley, she instantly said, "Mark, you need to find out more about Cartucho."

With the wonders of the modern internet now enabling instant access to the library of humanity, where any answer can be found to any imagined question, it didn't take too long to find all that was needed.

Barely a few days later, on a boat making a cup of tea, the tea bag in my hand caught my attention. It was vibrating subtly. At first, I presumed it was being caused by the boat's engine, but the boat was in dock and silent. The tremor was coming from within me.

Deep inside, I had finally connected the dots.

The realities of the incident, and the full significance of the events in Bogotá 1994, had come home to roost

THE SLUM DOGS OF CARTUCHO

In 1994, two main areas of Bogotá were notorious police no-go zones. The most famous was known as Cartucho, found to the south of the city centre. The name came from the recycling of cardboard and waste – the area's main industry. Consisting of several barricaded blocks, it was almost a walled city within a city, governed by its own laws and leaders. The name 'Cartucho' struck fear into the people of Bogotá.

The area of nearly twenty-three hectares and six hundred buildings was run by gangs who murdered anyone who crossed their path with impunity. Many of the inhabitants were submerged in the depths of abject poverty. Fuelled by addiction and infested by drug gangs, Cartucho became a cesspit of crime, and after several policemen were murdered here, the rest of the police force decided to stay away.

Back in 1994, when we had arrived at the airport, we had come across one policeman, maybe two.

The first of the police had been asleep in our taxi.

The second, who I think was police, had been manning the airport checkpoint. He had waved our driver through, failing to record our details, effectively priming us for the perfect disappearance.

If the taxi driver and team's plan had been simply to rob

us, we would have no doubt limped semi-naked into a police station that very night.

The missing passports alone would have started a chain of events that would have ended in the British and US consulates. Investigators could have easily pieced together our eyewitness accounts and could have traced the police on duty that night.

An identity parade would have confirmed their guilt, meaning careers were over and pensions cancelled. Low-down police facing loss of jobs and prison would have passed information on their superiors, bargaining for lighter sentences or amnesty.

This would have caused a domino effect, which was clearly far too risky for everyone involved. With a well-oiled 'disappearing' machine at hand, why let anyone survive the 'asset reallocation' to tell the tale?

It was easier, cheaper, and less risky to make sure no one could talk.

For each 'operation' that was left squeaky clean, the cycle could be repeated. The continuation meant, for all involved, at each level in the food chain, that the 'rewards' and backhanders would keep coming in.

Why would those involved – including members of the police – risk breaking that cycle?

The official records say 150,000 people went missing in Colombia during the early '90s.

Most of these people were victims of clashes between the government forces, FARC rebels and the drug gangs. These entities had the habit of burying their victims in unmarked graves.

If we had vanished in 1994, would the total number of people reported as missing be 150,002?

Of course not; the numbers are rounded to the nearest 10,000. That is how cheap life was, and still is.

During these days of the mid '90s in Bogotá, five homeless adults or street children were being 'socially cleansed' daily. Rogue police were easily hired as assassins. For the abandoned, the city became so dangerous that the street kids moved underground to live in the sewers. Not to be outwitted, the police resorted to pouring petrol down the city street manholes, burning the children alive.

It's easy to see how the poor barricaded themselves into 'police no-go' areas for safety, protecting themselves from the very people paid to protect them. Once these zones existed, they became magnets for the vulnerable. Desperation caused more crime, which set off a cascading downward spiral.

Although Cartucho was the most famous such area, there was another police no-go zone to the north of Bogotá called Bossa, also known as the Black Hole of Bogotá. Named as such because those caught in the vortexes of Bossa never came out.

Our driver left the airport and had tried to head north before I corrected him. This was the opposite way from the hotel, but directly towards Bossa. This taxi-driving night-time fisherman had to land his catch elsewhere.

If he'd been able to drop us with his normal disposal team, things would have moved at lightning speed. It would have been all over before we had a clue what was happening.

Within the alley he took us to, he had needed to slow,

looking for helpers he recognised. This gave the time I had needed to think, react and speak.

The infamous Cartucho was several blocks away. This alley was a mini franchise. I've posted some links to videos of Cartucho in the reference section at the back of this book. Images of people living amongst piles of rubbish. Some broken, bent double, others with backs straight and standing tall, ready to fight to live another day. The wild eyes of those traumatised and the empty gazes of those whose humanity had been forced out of them. These videos were shot in daylight.

Imagine these streets after midnight, devoid of street lighting.

Imagine these streets being the roads no cars went to except to drop off their cargo.

Then, you might get a glimpse of the real-life hell we had been driven into.

If the driver was looking for his team within the shadows of human beings coming towards us, it meant there were multiple reception squads. Each working for different gangs. This proves we were caught up in the mechanics of a well-worn routine.

A road with a single purpose.

A killing alley.

Occupied by reception committees.

Working for Bogotá's organised asset reallocation.

Men who 'disappeared' the living evidence of the crimes.

Ensuring perpetual silence.

The Slum Dogs of Cartucho.

Back to the present day, rather than researching in depth about the specific alleys, it's easier to track the history of their bigger cousins – the infamous hell holes that made international news.

The official police records recognise that 265 people vanished in Cartucho. The no-go area had been populated with impoverished and undocumented locals, rural migrants and outsiders.

Missing people can't be calculated unless it is known who was there in the first place.

Deaths cannot be calculated unless bodies are found.

The real number of deaths were clearly in the many thousands.

In the late nineties, as part of the general city-wide cleanup under a new mayor, the authorities regained control of Cartucho, evicting twelve thousand people. The buildings were bulldozed, and a park was built over the site in an attempt to wipe the slate of the city's memory clean.

Like a swarm of disturbed pigeons, the displaced of Cartucho regathered and settled nearby, forming what became a new hell hole called the Bronx.

The Bronx again become another slum city within a city,

that existed for fifteen devastating years until 2016. It took an invasion of two and a half thousand armed riot police to complete the task of clearing the slum.

Although the memory of the original Cartucho had been erased, the modern cameras and media of 2016 recorded the eviction and some of the findings.

The police unearthed the expected drug factories, brothels and child sex victims.

They found people who had been kidnapped endless evidence of torture, murder and what appeared to be Satanism.

Confirming the darkest conspiracy theories, they also discovered the Casas de Pique or the 'Chop Shops'. Rooms where the Butchers of Bogotá cut their victims up into small pieces, disposing of the evidence.

As they dug deep into the foundations, they found evidence of murder embedded in concrete .

Human skulls were found.

The police claimed they found sulphuric acid baths that had been used to dissolve the remains of the bodies.

I suspect that they invented this explanation, referencing the pseudo-romance of American noir detective novels to hide the grimmer realities and protect the country's image.

Why do I doubt it?

Acid costs money. It would have to be bought from specific and well-known suppliers, not the local 7-Eleven store.

The barrels would have been transported, leaving the equivalent of 'follow-me' chalk marks on the road for any inquiring investigator.

Mafia bosses in Britain famously kept pigs because they

eat everything, including bones. The absence of a body means no autopsy, which means no murder inquiry, which means they are simply missing. A 'missing person' notice might be generated, but who takes missing people seriously? They are just missing and might turn up, right?

Murder tactic number one: never let the body be found.

The Butchers of Bogotá dismembered bodies within their infamous chop houses.

But what did they do with the human meat and body parts afterwards?

Newspaper reports claimed the remains of murder victims were thrown into pits filled with alligators or fed to dogs.

Would this have happened to us?

I have little doubt that if I had not intervened, within three to thirty seconds later, our throats would have been cut.

It's strangely ironic that in complete naivety, I'd held a knife to our driver's throat, mimicking their intended actions.

In some sort of strange, Zen-like move, the force of aggression had been met with an equal yet opposite energy.

Had this set us free? Or was it the impact of the five words – or a combination of both?

Either way, if we hadn't managed to avoid the Butchers of Bogotá, I'm pretty sure the terror inflicted would have ended quickly.

We wouldn't have suffered too much.

These men were professionals.

I've lived amongst poor communities from India to sub-Saharan Africa and they are united by two highly visible factors.

Firstly, spotlessly clean children are sent to school dressed immaculately.

Secondly, nothing with the communities goes to waste.

In the West, we might consider something broken, but within the developing world, need and ingenuity means everything is mended or recycled, from broken flip-flops to plastic chairs.

Flip flops are retreaded with recalled tyres, and hot needles burn holes into cheap plastic chairs, enabling breaks to be threaded and repaired.

The same happens with food – nothing is wasted. The idea of special dog food is preposterous. In these poor communities, dogs survive on the leftovers. One way I've learnt to measure a village's subsistence levels is by the street dogs. Skinny dogs indicate a human community in need. Fat dogs suggest a plentiful supply of leftovers.

To the destitute, everything has a value. Everything that can be sold is sold. Anything that saves a dollar from being spent is a dollar saved.

When something is seen as expensive, cheaper options are found. I've witnessed beef burgers made of rat meat sold by street vendors in Malaysia and, shortly after the Wall came down, even at mobile burger stands within Poland's underground network.

Back in Bogotá, no one disputes the reason for, or existence of, the chop shops. My question is, once the bodies of the victims had been passed to the Butchers, what happened to the produce?

Cannibalism might seem far-fetched, but the people of Cartucho and the Bronx had been abandoned by the general society.

Those caught in extraordinary circumstances have been seen to do anything to survive. In 1972, Uruguayan flight 571 crashed high in the Andes mountains. Cold and hunger were killing the survivors of the crash one by one, leaving those left alive no other choice. One week, they were normal, middle-class, plane-ticket-buying passengers; the next week, they were cannibals.

A plane crash causing cannibalism might seem like a one-off.

In the 1930s, Stalin's head of the Secret Service proposed that the government resettle political undesirables. The Nazino colony was meant to achieve self-sufficiency in two years. However, thirteen weeks after its conception, the project failed spectacularly. Anarchy, violence and disease became rife in the community. When the authorities finally intervened, they discovered cannibalism and, to their horror, realised that 4,000 of the original deportees were dead or missing.

The events of World War Two also induced many such cases. Incidents ranged from civilians facing starvation within the sieges of Russian cities to German soldiers left on distant fronts devoid of supplies. These people were caught in extraordinary circumstances, with no other choice than to eat their own. Naturally, these tales of cannibalism were kept quiet from post-war civilian ears.

When death is close, previous morality becomes irrelevant. The choice becomes holding onto previously held ethics and dying or adapting to circumstances and living. After a while, everything that once seemed horrific quickly becomes an everyday normality.

The Rio police assassin explained it to me clearly. Killing his first child left him feeling queasy. With some practice, his semi-licensed serial killing left him feeling no different than as if he'd just extinguished some rodents.

London of the 19th century is remembered for the body snatchers that either robbed fresh graves or killed to get bodies to sell to universities for medical experiments and dissection – true stories from Britain's 19th century that still keep the audiences of horror entertained today with countless books and films.

Cities and countries go through stages of development.

In Barranquilla, Colombia, homeless waste collector Oscar Hemandez was lured to a local university with the promise of being given cardboard for recycling. Along with several others, he was clubbed and left for dead in a tub of formaldehyde. He regained consciousness, escaped and made his way to the authorities.

The police raided the university and found the bodies of

twelve homeless people and body pieces belonging to another eleven in the medical department's morgue. The university's security men later admitted to killing fifty other homeless people for the university's director, in return for a two-hundred-dollar bounty per victim. This happened in 1992.

A dead body has value. Whole, dissected, or butchered.

One thing is for sure.

Two sets of foreign passports, cash, traveller's cheques and bags full of possessions would have seemed like a gold mine.

In the early nineties, human life was cheap in Colombia at $200 a head.

One of our passports enabling someone to start a new life in the UK or USA was worth $2,000 on the black market.

$2,000 was also the cost for 50 homeless people to be murdered so that medical students could practice dissection.

It's interesting to note the difference in terms here.

Medical students are seen to dissect a body, in stark contrast to the image of the Butchers of Bogotá chopping up victims.

One group seen as at the top of society, and one at the bottom, yet both were 'working' on murder victims.

Those higher up the thieves' food chain would have taken the cash and the British and American passports. The next down the food chain would have taken the electronics and clothes. The next tier would have taken our shoes, socks, and even underwear. Nothing would have been wasted.

Then, at the bottom of the food chain of the asset-reallocators, lay the Butchers of Bogotá.

Who were these people?

Were the jobs needed to work the taxi scam divided up equally by the gang leaders, or did they take turns?

"Alright, gang. This evening, I'll do the taxi driving. Pedro, you slit the throats, and... don't frown, Jose... yes, it's your turn to do the butchering. And Jose, listen to me. This week I want to see nicely cut, thin rump steaks. Not that hack-job you did last week!"

The Butchers will have come from those most desperate. No one will have volunteered for this.

I'd met Luciana's brother in the comparatively heavenly El Barrio of Ecuador's Guayaquil, working as a drug courier paid not in cash but with crack. We witnessed up close how his life was hanging by a thread.

Would someone whose life had already descended to the level of chopping up human bodies feed the produce of his work to dogs, when disguised meat could be swapped for money or drugs?

Is it possible that the Butchers of Bogotá's produce was sold cheaply to street vendors?

Vendors that were probably themselves desperate addicts, who were then able to sell cut-price street food to the desperate slum population?

A method easier and cheaper than using acid baths, that earned money instead of wasting cash on barrels of acid.

And who could keep a pet alligator in a slum? Surely only drug lords fancying themselves as James Bond villains would have the resources to look after such a creature.

Besides, who could tell the difference between a beef rib-eye steak and a tender cut of human rump steak?

The impoverished and drug addicts would have happily

bought dirt-cheap chilli-con-carne, or pork tacos, not questioning or knowing the source.

Basic body parts would have been easy to disguise, yet skulls, teeth and jawbones would have given the game away.

Everyone would recognise a human skull.

The ultimate taboo.

The skulls needed to be disposed of in a different manner, hence many bodiless skulls were found buried under the chop houses.

If cannibalism had been documented, would there be an easily accessible public record that we could access now?

It is not hard to imagine the police, army and city officials responsible for rebuilding a traumatised society choosing to sweep such incidents under the carpet.

I must be clear that the above is a theory, not proven in any way.

The only way to learn more would be to dig deeper by returning to Bogotá and finding an eye witness to the killing alleys or chop shops.

Maybe, one day, I will.

Or maybe, like the city mayors, I'll let the story rest, relegating these nightmares of the past to the history books, instead dreaming of happier futures where wealth and abundance are distributed equally.

To sum it all up, what do I believe would have happened if the driver had not pressed the accelerator to the floor?

I have little doubt.

To use a British expression, we would have been toast.

Or minced meat.

Or maybe repackaged as pork chops?

More realistically, 'traveller-con-carne' street-food style.

If we believe the official narrative, we'd have become dog food.

Or, more exotically, alligator snacks.

Or dissolved in acid.

Or, maybe, more boringly, just dismembered and buried.

Whichever way, you wouldn't have got to read this *world-wild travel tale*, '3 Seconds in Bogotá'.

Did the knife persuade him?

Or, was it the five magic words?

If a pen is mightier than a sword, are spoken words mightier than a blade?

"No quiero no problemas, señor."

The words, even though from my mouth, still haunt me, and maybe, they still haunt him.

"I don't want any problems, sir."

Imagine a life without problems.

Probably.

Like you.

Like me.

All he ever wanted.

Was less problems.

Across the divide.

Of the rich and the poor.

The words connected us.

My dream.

His dream.

Our dream.

END NOTE FROM AUTHOR

If you'd like to send a message, ask a question, or have further
research to send,
please use this email:
mark@markplayne.com

If you'd like to keep in touch and hear about new books,
join my author list:
markplayne.co.uk/join

BIBLIOGRAPHY

If you're interested in any of the events or subjects mentioned
within
3 Seconds in Bogotá
or the epilogue
Stories Behind the Stories
I've collated these following references
to help kickstart your research.

The references are split into two sections.

1 - References to events and places mentioned within
3 Seconds in Bogotá

2- References to the research within the Epilogue Stories
behind the Stories.

Both sections are easy to access with the member's area:
markplayne.co.uk/123)

g

REFERENCES - 3 SECONDS IN BOGOTÁ

Chapter 2 - 1994

27 Club

- **Wikipedia:** https://en.wikipedia.org/wiki/27_Club
- **Article:** https://www.smoothradio.com/news/music/27-club-members/

Chapter 5 - The Fine Art of Bad Spanish

Floods in Mina Clavero Argentina

The runoffs in the mountains are better managed now, yet when the rains come, the river of Mina Clavero still floods. This modern footage gives an idea of what we witnessed.

- **Floods caught on camera**: https://www.youtube.com/watch?v=-JfvAnGD7gI

See videos here: markplayne.co.uk/321

Chapter 7 - Impossibly Possible

- **Guinea Pig recipe and a famous painting**: https://www.alpacaexpeditions.com/guinea-pig-recipe/
- **Wikipedia - Cuzco stone walls**: https://en.wikipedia.org/wiki/Twelve-angled_stone
- **Theories behind the stone walls**: https://www.youtube.com/watch?v=XwDRZ-u8E2Q&list=ULAohxBVuDHxw&index=534

See videos here: markplayne.co.uk/321

- **Coca leaves to combat altitude sickness**: https://link.springer.com/article/10.1186/s40794-019-0095-7

Chapter 8 - Apples, Bullets and Beer

Wayne Bobbit

Yes, this is real! She chopped it off...

- **Wikipedia:** https://en.wikipedia.org/wiki/John_and_Lorena_Bobbitt
- **TV series on Amazon:** https://amzn.to/2VtqMVF
- **NY Times newspaper report:** https://www.nytimes.com/2019/01/30/arts/television/lorena-bobbitt-documentary-jordan-peele.html

Chapter 11 - Loosing My Religion

Madres de Plaza de Mayo

Once considered a conspiracy theory, this is important history on many levels.

- **Wikipedia:** Wikipedia
- **Women in World History:** http://www.womeninworldhistory.com/contemporary-07.html
- **Vamos Spanish:** https://vamospanish.com/discover/madres-plaza-mayo-mothers-argentina/
- **The Guardian**: https://www.theguardian.com/world/2017/apr/28/mothers-plaza-de-mayo-argentina-anniversary

Chapter 11 - Loosing My Religion

Falklands war

"In war, truth is the first casualty."

Aeschylus

"...Naturally, the common people don't want war but after all it is the leaders of a country who determine the policy, and it is always a simple matter to drag the people along, whether it is a democracy, or a fascist dictatorship, or a parliament, or a communist dictatorship. Voice or no voice, the people can always be brought to the bidding of the leaders. That is easy. All you have to do is to tell them they are being attacked, and denounce the pacifists for lack of patriotism and exposing the country to danger. It works the same in every country..."

Hermann Goring

- **Wikipedia:** https://en.wikipedia.org/wiki/ Falklands_War
- **Independent's Falkland war photographs:** https://www.independent.co.uk/

life-style/history/falklands-war-a-look-back-in-50-
photographs-7581454.html

- **The Guardian on Thatcher and the
  Falklands:** https://www.theguardian.com/
  politics/2013/apr/09/margaret-thatcher-
  falklands-gambleThatcher and Falklands
- **UPI news: Was the sinking of the
  Belgrano illegal?** https://www.upi.com/
  Archives/2000/06/30/Thatcher-being-sued-over-
  Falklands-war/5478962337600/

One click links at: markplayne.co.uk/321

Chapter 11 - Loosing My Religion

Foz do Iguacu

Immense waterfalls that straddle three nations. Unmissable.

- **Spectacular modern drone footage:**
  Drone footage https://www.youtube.com/watch?
  v=Jt9X8fCmRw4

See videos here: markplayne.co.uk/321

Chapter 11 - Loosing My Religion

Kurt Cobain

Suicide or murder? The disputed 'Soaked in Bleach' documentary makes an interesting case for the latter.

- **Soaked in Bleach:** https://amzn.to/34Tje1q
- **Independent Newspaper. Kurt Cobain's murder questioned:** https://www.independent.co.uk/arts-entertainment/music/features/kurt-cobain-death-suicide-anniversary-nirvana-courtney-love-theories-manager-interview-a8854766.html

Chapter 11 - Loosing My Religion

Jimi Hendrix

Questions surround Hendrix's death.

- **Wikipedia**: https://en.wikipedia.org/wiki/Death_of_Jimi_Hendrix
- **Independent Newspaper. Hendrix murdered by manager?** https://www.independent.co.uk/news/people/news/hendrix-murdered-by-his-manager-says-former-aide-1693583.html
- **The Hendrix conspiracy:** http://woodstockstory.com/jimi-hendrix-murdered-conspiracy.htmlWoodstockstory
- **Doctor's report produces questions:** https://constantinereport.com/attending-

physician-jimi-hendrix-was-waterboarded-to-
death-w-red-wine/
- **How did Hendrix die?** https://
curiosityaroused.com/culture/how-did-jimi-
hendrix-die/

One click links at: markplayne.co.uk/321

Chapter 11 - Loosing My Religion

Shooting of Street Kids in Latin America
WARNING. Graphic photos and footage.

- **Recent documented shootings:** *"They
(Police) say: "We don't go into favelas to die. We go
in there to kill."* https://cyberwarzone.com/street-
kids-murdered-clean-brazil-ahead-world-cup/
- **Shooting caught on camera**: https://
jonathanturley.org/2011/03/25/shock-video-
brazilian-police-shown-shooting-unarmed-child-
in-chest/

Chapter 13 - Turkish delight

Goröme - Cappadoccia Turkey

One of the natural wonders of the world.
Highly recommended.

- **Spectacular drone footage:** https://www.youtube.com/watch?v=f3lv65BFmaA

See videos here: markplayne.co.uk/321

'PASEO MILLONARIO'

The 'taxi scam' that has continued on and been adapted since the early '90s.

Even recently with the internet, widespread surveillance and every customer having a mobile phone, enabling them to take and send photos and call for help, the robberies continue.

The City Paper 2013

"...In Bogotá, security is an important aspect of daily life, and one of the most notorious methods of robbery known as 'paseo millonario,' involves pirate taxis orchestrating a route, **which under the best of circumstances results in armed robbery**..."

"...If you should suspect something worrisome

within minutes of taking a cab, the most important advice is to stay calm. When a potential victim gets angry, restless and aggressive, they can be harmed. Such was the case of 36-year-old Russian Vitaly Shubinsky, whose body was found in the south of Bogotá in July 2012, after he took a cab from the 93 Park..."

"...even passengers arriving on flights into the new El Dorado Airport should be very cautious only to take licensed cabs, even if the lines are long at the taxi dispatch. While El Dorado has CCTV, the best guarantee for a safe ride is to wait curbside in the official line..."

- STORIES BEHIND THE STORIES - REFERENCES & LINKShttps://thecitypaperbogota.com/bogota/paseo-millonario-a-dangerous-ride/2192

One click links at: markplayne.co.uk/321

* * *

SPECIAL AGENT WATSON

DEA website Sept 2014

> *"...Gracia Ramirez admitted that he and his conspirators agreed to conduct a "paseo milionario" or "millionaire's ride" in which victims who were perceived as wealthy were lured into taxi cabs, kidnapped and then robbed. Gracia Ramirez admitted that he targeted Special Agent Watson and picked him up outside a Bogotà restaurant in his taxi. Soon after, two conspirators entered Gracia Ramirez's taxi, and one used a stun gun to shock Special Agent Watson and the other stabbed him. Special Agent Watson was able to escape from the taxi, but he later collapsed and died from his injuries..."*

- https://www.dea.gov/press-releases/2014/09/04/colombian-national-pleads-guilty-kidnapping-and-murder-dea-agent-terry

Officer Down Memorial page

> *"...Special Agent Terry Watson was stabbed to death in Bogota, Colombia..."*

- https://www.odmp.org/officer/21937-special-agent-james-terry-watson

If you didn't see these before, to get a sense of *Cartucho* and the other police no-go areas, check the superb collection of black and white photos by Stanislas Guigi.

- http://stanislasguigui.com/en/portfolio-25634-0-40-calle-del-cartucho.html

One click links at: markplayne.co.uk/321

* * *

CARTUCHO

Documentary film '*Cartucho*'

Ex-resident and body collector says 1000s buried under the new park where Cartucho was before demolition. Below is the trailer for the film festival documentary.

- https://vimeo.com/251402826

See videos here: markplayne.co.uk/321

Expat chronicles 2014

"...Several police were killed there, and on some occasions grenades were thrown by the mafia soldiers. When police were no longer willing to enter El Cartucho, they erected roadblock barricades and guarded the borders. Laws inside were dictated by the traffickers. While there are no statistics given homicide victims were internally disposed of, the murder rate in El Cartucho was higher than in Iraq or the former Yugoslavia during their respective wars. In enforcing the gangs' street code, there were murders every day. The mafia soldiers were an integral part of life in El Cartucho as they maintained order in the kingdom of thieves and addicts. Stories abound of bodies being quartered with chainsaws and buried under the blocks of El Cartucho..."

- https://expat-chronicles.com/2014/12/21/el-cartucho-bogota/

* * *

THE BRONX

When Cartucho was demolished in the late nineties, the area reformed itself nearby in the smaller area known as the Bronx.

Since this was in existence recently there is more material available for research.

The City Bogotá Paper - June 2017

"...The truth is, that for most of Bogotá, El Bronx, was the ghoulish "Independent Crime Republic" as Mayor Peñalosa referred to it, where drug dealing and child prostitution went unchecked. Then, evidence of torture, murder and dismemberment in so-called 'chop houses' in which the dead were fed to starving dogs, or buried under the concrete floors. Despite the fear, the mere mention of El Bronx generated in the minds of Bogotanos, the horror filled just four streets..." Read more:

- https://thecitypaperbogota.com/bogota/el-bronx-a-virtual-journey-to-hell-continues-online/17314

Rueters

"...When around 2,500 heavily armed police and soldiers recently raided a warren of crack dens in a notorious Bogota neighborhood to tackle drug trafficking, they also found two hundred children being used as sex slaves..."

- https://www.reuters.com/article/us-colombia-humantrafficking-idUSKCN0YN5H0

One click links at: markplayne.co.uk/321

* * *

BOSSA
'The Black Hole of Bogotá'

LA Times 2006

"...A decade ago, the Bosa slum was the black hole of Bogota. Its darkest corner was Laurel Park, a grassless, trash-strewn lot with open sewage and gun-toting gangs bent on muggings and murder..."

- https://www.latimes.com/archives/la-xpm-2006-oct-28-fg-bogota28-story.html

One click links at: markplayne.co.uk/321

* * *

LAS CASAS DE PIQUE
The Chop Houses

Colombia Reports 2016

"...Evidence of torture chambers found blocks away from Colombia's presidential palace...the discovery of so-called "chop-up houses" in the port city of Buenaventura, similar torture and dismemberment chambers have been found in Medellin, and now in Bogota. The first reports on homes that had been abandoned and converted into torture and dismemberment chambers...were used to dismember homicide victims after which the remains were thrown in the Pacific Ocean. The gruesome practice hit the international headlines again in 2015 when Medellin police found evidence of similar horror homes inside government-financed housing projects in the Urabeños-controled west of the city and in abandoned warehouses downtown..."

- https://colombiareports.com/keep-colombias-homicide-rate-low-dismember-dispose-victims-remains/

The Guardian 2014

"...The criminals recruit children, extort businesses, force people from their homes and dismember live victims, scattering their remains in the bay or

surrounding jungle. Dozens of wooden huts balanced precariously on stilts over the bay have been abandoned by terrorised citizens and taken over by the gangs for use as casas de pique, or chop houses, where they torture and murder their victims..."

- https://www.theguardian.com/world/2014/oct/ 12/colombia-violence-torture-gangs-buenaventura

Chop Houses in the Bronx
City Lab 2018

"...Described as "a living hell" by Colombian newspapers, as many as 3,000 people lived in the streets, which were controlled by a heavily-armed gang of micro-traffickers known as "Sayayines," who sent anyone who crossed their path to the Casa de Pique [chop house].

Bodies were disposed of by crocodiles kept in basements; a 100-meter long underground tunnel was used to smuggle drugs, weapons, and kidnap victims in and out; underage girls were kept as sex slaves; and torture rooms were equipped with the most macabre of instruments..."

- https://www.citylab.com/life/2018/03/bogotas- bronx-is-barren-but-not-for-long/556535/

One click links at: markplayne.co.uk/321

* * *

BRONX ON CAMERA

The Bronx raid of 2500 police on camera. 2016

Video using body cam footage of the police.
This video is in Spanish.
Turn auto-translate on to your language.

- They found the chop houses.
- Victims fed to dogs and crocodiles.
- Footage shows the rescue of one boy before he was to be killed.
- The journalist says the mafia controlling here had infiltrated the police and were paying high bribes.
- They offered huge bounties for the bodies of dead police.

See the raid here:

- https://www.youtube.com/watch?v= wJDmlCPPKlY

Watch all videos here: markplayne.co.uk/321

3-minute expose in the Bronx

Kidnapping, torture and satanism

- Evidence of chop shops.
- Body parts in concrete.
- Rooms where people have clearly been shot against wall.

- https://www.youtube.com/watch?v= 8iyDykDd55Q

Watch all videos here: markplayne.co.uk/321

Los Sayayines, el comando armado ilegal que por años sembró terror en el Bronx.

- The Sayayines, the illegal armed gangs that for years controlled the Bronx with terror.
- Surveillance videos show people dragging dead bodies in broad daylight

- https://www.youtube.com/watch?v= 20CaoSZqHN8

See videos here: markplayne.co.uk/321

* * *

STREET KIDS

Street kids looked after by charity. 2019

"...Most children living in Bogotá's sewers do not want to leave. They grow accustomed to the waist-deep feces, the stench, the darkness, the water and the rats. As frightening and dangerous as the sewers are, the children feel safe there..."

- https://www.deseret.com/2019/8/24/20829120/lds-humanitarian-missionaries-colombia-children-bogota-latin-america-tour-russell-m-nelson-latam

LA Times: The Sewer Kids of Bogota

"...Underground : Hundreds of young vagrants live desperate, stoned lives in the storm sewers under Colombia's capital. They gather there for protection from the elements, and from vigilante hit squads who threaten their very lives..."

- https://www.latimes.com/archives/la-xpm-1990-11-06-wr-3939-story.html

CNN - Sewers home to vagrant Colombian kids

"...The sewage system running under Bogota's streets was filled with packs of kids living waist-deep in human waste and taking in copious amounts of glue and crack in order to cope.

This was at the height of Colombia's Dirty War, and the whole reason street kids had moved into the sewers in the first place was to get away from the violence above ground. But then the paramilitary death squads who had chased them off the street started coming into the pipes and shooting them or dousing them in gasoline or raping them.

The sewer kids became a fairly big humanitarian story in the media for a while, with networks in America and Europe sending in TV crews to cover it and folks setting up charities abroad. Then, as happens with news stories, it fell off the radar, and I guess people kind of thought the problem had been resolved, if they thought of it at all.

But what had actually happened was, about six months after all the stories aired, the death squads went in, armed with the whereabouts of the sewer-kid hot spots, and carried out massive reprisal killings. There was some talk in the government about cracking down on the death squads, but by all accounts, soldiers and off-duty cops made up a good part of most squads. So the situation just stagnated while the world turned its attention elsewhere..."

- https://edition.cnn.com/2010/WORLD/
  americas/04/22/vbs.sewers.bogota/index.html

* * *

DESPERATION

Flight 571 Crash Andes 1972

Wikipedia

"...During the next 72 days, 13 more passengers died. The remaining survivors reluctantly resorted to eating the dead..."

- https://en.wikipedia.org/wiki/
  Uruguayan_Air_Force_Flight_571

WW2
Picture History

"...Many instances of cannibalism by necessity were recorded during World War II. For example, during the 872-day Siege of Leningrad, reports of cannibalism began to appear in the winter of 1941–1942, after all birds, rats and pets were eaten by survivors.

Leningrad police even formed a special division to combat cannibalism. Following the Soviet victory at Stalingrad it was found that some German soldiers in the besieged city, cut off from supplies, resorted to cannibalism..."

- https://pictureshistory.blogspot.com/2010/08/ cannibalism-during-second-world-war.html

The Nazino Affair & the Cannibals of Death Island

"...Shortly after the settlers arrived on Nazino, Stalin finally rejected the idea of the labor settlements. However, on May 27, a further 1200 deportees joined the original settlers on Nazino. By this time order had well and truly broken down, with death, disease, and chaos in charge. Those settlers with a flour ration found that without utensils and bread ovens, there was no way they could bake bread. In desperation, they mixed their flour rations with river water and quickly contracted dysentery. Many, already weak died. However, some managed to escape illness. For them, there were just two choices.

The first choice was to escape. Some of the more able settlers constructed makeshift rafts and tried to escape by the river. Many drowned when the rafts came apart midstream. Others who survived the water found themselves hunted down like animals for the sport of the guards. However, anyone who made it across the water was left unmolested. This was because the terrain was so harsh and the escapees so ill-prepared for survival that they were deemed as good as dead.

*The second choice was to stay on Nazino and survive whatever the cost. Murder became frequent as the survivors fought over the meager and ever diminishing resources. The guards were unable to control the gangs, which roamed the island and so left them to their murderous rampages, contenting themselves with punishing minor offenses amongst the weaker individuals. However, by the end of the first week, the starving settlers had already **turned to cannibalism**. The signs were first noticed by health officers who observed five corpses with body parts missing..."*

- https://historycollection.com/the-nazino-affair-the-tragedy-of-cannibal-island/

One click links at: markplayne.co.uk/321

* * *

MURDERED IN THE NAME OF MEDICINE
The Body Snatchers

AP news 1992

"...Twenty-two bodies found in a university morgue appear to be the gruesome harvest of a ring that kills homeless people to sell their cadavers to medicine, police say..."

- https://apnews.com/
  c5f2d6deeaf316e90e592abf8fcbcd1e

EASY ACCESS TO REFERENCES VIA AUTHOR'S WEBSITE

As mentioned all the previous references, links and videos
referring to things mentioned within
3 Seconds in Bogotá
and research leading the theories within the
Epilogue
can easily be found within
the member's area on the author's website.
markplayne.co.uk/321

This section of the website is often updated with any new
research and relevant videos.

SUGGESTED FURTHER READING.

American Made

By Shaun Attwood

Shaun Attwood's true story and investigation into the war on drugs is a compelling read.

If, after reading *3 Seconds in Bogotá,* you're wondering about the backdrop that created such poverty that in turn produced such atrocities, this is the next book to read.

Who was really behind the explosion in cocaine use in the USA?

Find out with this key book from Shaun's series on the 'War on Drugs'.

American Made is the jaw-dropping true story of CIA drug-smuggling pilot Barry Seal that the Hollywood movie starring Tom Cruise was afraid to tell.

Highly recommended and guaranteed to blow your mind.
SHOP: https://geni.us/American-Made

Marching Powder.

By Rusty Young

Maybe the most-read book by travellers of South America.

Brit Thomas McFadden was busted for drug smuggling in Bolivia and ended up living a surreal prison life, even conducting prison tours for travellers who had heard of his plight.

> *Thomas ended up making a living by giving backpackers tours of the prison – he became a fixture on the back-packing circuit and was named in the Lonely Planet guide to Bolivia. When he was told that for a bribe of $5000 his sentence could be overturned, it was the many backpackers who'd passed through who sent him the money. Written by lawyer Rusty Young, Marching Powder – sometimes shocking, sometimes funny – is a riveting story of survival.*

Amazon: https://geni.us/Marching-Powder

* * *

Shantaram

By Gregory David Roberts

This is a must-read for all travellers, especially those already there, or planning to go to India.

This is a beautifully told 'true story' of an Aussie on the run who melted away from sight into Mumbai's underbelly, learning the workings of the mafia, Bollywood and the slum life.

Great insights into the people and country.

Unmissable.

Now on Netflix.

'In the early 8os, Gregory David Roberts, an armed robber and heroin addict, escaped from an Australian prison to India, where he lived in a Bombay slum. There, he established a free health clinic and also joined the mafia, working as a money launderer, forger and street soldier. He found time to learn Hindi and Marathi, fall in love, and spend time being worked over in an Indian jail. Then, in case anyone thought he was slacking, he acted in Bollywood and fought with the Mujahedeen in Afghanistan... Amazingly, Roberts wrote Shantaram three times after prison guards trashed the first two versions. It's a profound tribute to his willpower... At once a high-kicking, eye-gouging

adventure, a love saga and a savage yet tenderly lyrical fugitive vision.' Time Out

---

Amazon: https://geni.us/Shantaram

* * *

Other independent travel writers you might like…

- Adam Fletcher
- Mark Walters
- Kathryn Bonella
- George Mahood
- Yossi Ghinsberg
- Paul Wilson

Quick easy links to everything:
markplayne.co.uk/321

DEDICATIONS

To my loved ones.
For your endless patience and eternal support.
You know who you are :)

also

To my Mother, and all mothers,
for their unwavering love
for their wayward sons.

not forgetting

The 150,000+ that were 'disappeared'
during those troubled years.

God bless you.

ACKNOWLEDGEMENTS

EDITING
Sonia Ferreira
Gill Davies
Helen Baggott
Rosemary Lawton
Suzy Azar

SUPPORT
Jos Bakker
Francesca Haywood
Kim Hawksley
Fiona Pinscher
Lizzie Chadwick
Jon Collins
Åse Lejbølle
Polly Lyndle
Philip Haywood
Lynsey Doel

YOUR OPINON MATTERS

If you can spare a moment, please leave an honest review on
your favourite online bookstore
and/or
Goodreads.

**If you love physical books and appreciate this
title,
please mention
or ask your local independent bookstore or
library
to stock
'3 Seconds in Bogotá'**

Paperback ISBN: 9781739325428
Hardback ISBN: 9781739325435

WHY LEAVE A REVIEW?

As a reader, your opinion matters more than you might realise. When you take the time to write a review of a book, you are providing valuable feedback to the author and are helping them reach a wider audience.

By sharing your thoughts and opinions, you are helping other potential readers decide whether or not the book is worth their time and money. Your review can also help to boost the book's visibility, making it easier for the book to gain traction in a crowded marketplace and reach new readers.

Additionally, writing a review is an opportunity to engage with not only the author, but the larger literary community.

It allows you to share your insights and perspectives, connect with like-minded readers, and participate in ongoing conversations about literature.

Your review will also help to shape the larger cultural conversation around a book, contributing to a broader understanding of its themes, characters, and ideas. So, we urge you to take a few moments to write a review after finishing this book.

Your feedback can have a significant impact on an author's career and on the broader literary landscape, making it a small but powerful way to make a difference in the world of books.

JOIN AUTHOR'S NEWSLETTER

Would you like to read and hear more from Mark Playne and access special editions and updates?

Join his newsletter
Markplayne.co.uk/join

Published by Wild Tales - Bath, United Kingdom
Cover design: Abe Rsmana

1st edition – Published 5th April 2019
2nd edition – Published 11th July 2019
3rd Edition – Published 20th Feb 2020
4th Edition with Epilogue – Published 3rd Feb 2023
Paperback ISBN: 9781739325428
Hardback ISBN: 9781739325435
For other language versions visit Markplayne.co.uk